Our teams combed the wreckage, unsure where people would be found. Every now and then the teams would call for a "quiet" in some isolated section. A company officer would silence everyone working that area. Radios would be turned down. Like dozens of times before, the team leader would cry out to anyone within earshot: "Hey, make a noise! We are police officers and firefighters. Where are you?" Everybody would pause and strain to hear a response. They would shift positions, placing their ears down next to the debris itself.

Then they would shout into the rubble at the top of their lungs. "Hey, we're here to help you! Call out to us. . . . *Please*." It was almost as if rescue workers were trying to will the survivors to live.

Then silence again. More waiting. Everyone was praying in their own way that we would hear a sound, any sound. We longed to hear a whisper or a sob or a tapping on the concrete that surrounded us. We strained our senses, already heightened by our deep desire to find someone, anyone.

Occasionally it happened. We got a response. And when we did, emotion spread like wildfire through the entire building. Unfortunately, it didn't happen as often as we hoped. But when it did, the victory was felt by all. . . .

OKLAHOMA RESCUE

Jon Hansen

LIZ,
THANK YOU FOR YOUR
HELP & SUPPORT!
TAKE CARE & God BLESS

Jon Hansen
3/13/96

BALLANTINE BOOKS • NEW YORK

Copyright © 1995 by Jon Hansen

All rights reserved under International and Pan-American Copyright Conventions. Published in the United States by Ballantine Books, a division of Random House, Inc., New York, and simultaneously in Canada by Random House of Canada Limited, Toronto.

Background cover photo copyright © by Reuters/Bettman Archives
Cover photo of Jon Hansen copyright © by Hi-Shots International 1995

ISBN 0-345-40252-3

Manufactured in the United States of America

First Edition: June 1995

10 9 8 7 6 5 4 3

To the victims—those who survived and those who perished—as well as their families and loved ones.

To all the men and women of the Oklahoma City Fire Department, the Oklahoma City Police Department, the Oklahoma County Sheriff's Office, the Oklahoma Highway Patrol, Emergency Medical Services Authority, Medical Examiner's Office, Oklahoma National Guard, Tinker Air Force Base personnel and all other involved military units, the Federal Emergency Management Agency and their Urban Search And Rescue teams, metro area and state public safety agencies, and the countless volunteers who kept us going . . . for their time, their spirit, and their compassion.

To the families of these many individuals who so unselfishly lent them to us.

To my own family for their ongoing love and support: Jenifer, Cory, Jill, and Dad.

Contents

Acknowledgments

I appreciate the efforts of all those who helped me pay tribute to the brave men and women of all the public safety agencies locally and from across the country with this publication.

I want to thank Mary Myrick, who approached me with this idea and managed the project; Linda Grey and Joe Blades from Ballantine Books; Susan Rawls, Linda Richardson, Richard and Patty Labarthe, Steve Graham, Richard Zahn, Kevin McAfee, Craig Rolke, Danny Atchley, Mike Shannon; Terry Phillips from Hi-Shots International; and *The Daily Oklahoman* for their work in making it happen.

I thank Commander Doug (Hound Dog) McClain, Chris Neal, Anthony McDermid, Dave Grider, Stewart Meyer, David Hackett, Jim Johnson, Brent Gravel, Carl Whittle, Bruce Watkins, Jack Smiley, Ted Wilson, and my friends at the Oklahoma City Fire Department for their help and support in tough times.

Acknowledgments

* * *

Thanks to Federal Emergency Management Agency director James Lee Witt and all the Urban Search And Rescue teams involved for your quick response, hard work, and insightful guidance. Thanks to Chief Ray Downey, Chief Mark Ghillarducci, and Chief Dennis Compton for their efforts in coordinating FEMA's operations here. I look forward to continuing the friendships that we have developed for many years to come.

Thanks to the staff and instructors at Oklahoma State University's Fire Service Training, the National Fire Academy, the Emergency Management Institute, and other training facilities for imparting the knowledge and skills that enabled us to perform our jobs so well.

I thank all the rescuers, medical professionals, caregivers, clergy, service providers, and behind-the-scenes supporters—too numerous to name—for the impressive way in which everyone worked together so smoothly regardless of which organization or group they represented.

Thanks to the American Red Cross, the Salvation Army, and the many other organizations who specialize in disaster relief.

I thank all of our leaders: Governor and Mrs. Frank Keating, Lieutenant Governor Mary Fallin, Mayor Ron Norick and our City Council, City

Acknowledgments

Manager Don Bown, Assistant City Manager Joevan Bullard, Fire Chief Gary Marrs, Police Chief Sam Gonzales, Adjutant General Steve Cortright, Oklahoma Commissioner of Public Safety Kenneth Vanhoy, State Medical Examiner Dr. Fred Jordan, Director of Civil Emergency Management Tom Feuerborn, Emergency Medical Services' Medical Director Dr. Peter Maningas, Oklahoma City Firefighters Association President Charlie Stone, Oklahoma County District Attorney Bob Macy, and the many state, local, and federal elected officials.

I thank the media for their cooperation and patience as we all worked together to keep the world informed.

I thank the many companies who provided all the supplies and services we relied on, especially Southwestern Bell Telephone Company, who allowed us to set up our permanent command center inside their corporate headquarters at One Bell Central. My appreciation also goes to both Southwestern Bell Mobile Systems and Cellular One for making our communications work so well.

Thanks to Dad for setting the example, to Jenifer for being there for me, to Cory for being my "bud," to Jill for a fresh outlook on life, and to Norene, Kathy, and Annie for helping.

* * *

Acknowledgments

A special thanks to Bob and Debbie Pippin, the Thompson family, Aren Almon, Kenneth Adams, and Curtis Froh—watching you face this tragedy with courage and class set an inspirational example for us all.

My sincere appreciation goes to my fellow three and a half million citizens whose generosity and compassion showed the world our true Oklahoma spirit.

My deepest gratitude goes to the many people across the country and around the world who kept all of us in their hearts and in their prayers.

And, finally, I thank *all* the men and women of the Oklahoma City Fire Department who continue to serve and to shine!

THE AREA SURROUNDING THE ALFRED P. MURRAH
BUILDING IN DOWNTOWN OKLAHOMA CITY

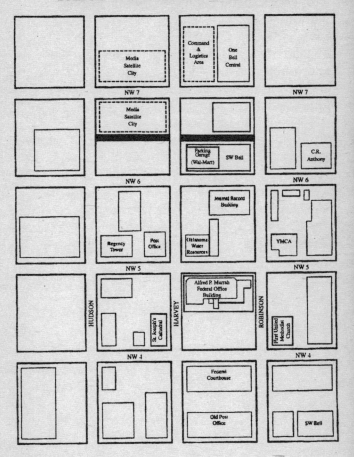

Prologue

T HIS IS A story of ordinary Americans responding to a national crisis with extraordinary compassion, bravery, and dedication. So perhaps it is only fitting that I preface their story with the wisdom of an ordinary American who led his country through its gravest crisis with those very same qualities.

During his presidency, Abraham Lincoln attended church near the White House, slipping in with one of his aides after the service began to hear the sermon and leaving early so that his presence wouldn't disrupt the congregation.

One evening as they were leaving the church, the aide asked President Lincoln what he thought of the sermon. Lincoln thought for some time before giving his answer. "Well, I must say that the content was excellent, and Dr. Gurley certainly preached with eloquence. You could tell that he had really put a lot of work into his sermon."

"So, you liked it? You thought it was a great sermon?" asked the aide.

And Lincoln replied, "No, I didn't say that."

"You said the sermon was excellent," countered the aide.

"That's true," replied Lincoln, "but I didn't say it was a great sermon."

"Well what's the difference?" asked the aide.

Lincoln's answer was profound. He said, "Dr. Gurley forgot the most important ingredient of all. He failed to ask us to do something great."

On April 19, 1995, Oklahoma City became the site of the most deadly terrorist act in our nation's history. The country was shocked that this horrible demonstration of violence could happen in the Heartland of America. People were equally amazed by the community's response.

This is the proud story of Oklahomans, who without waiting to be asked, did something great They responded to the tragedy by giving of themselves to ease the pain and suffering their community was forced to experience. It's a story straight from the Heartland—and from the heart

1

Prepared for Disaster

T WENTY-TWO YEARS IN the fire service will teach
you to be ready for anything. But on April 19,
1995, I learned there are some things you can
never be completely ready to face. You can be
prepared—and that helps—but you can never totally be ready for a disaster of this magnitude.

It was just after nine A.M. when I heard the explosion. It shook my entire office building five
blocks away. Ceiling tiles fell. Pictures rattled on
the walls. I almost dropped the phone. I was talking with a local TV reporter at the time about
plans for an upcoming citywide public service
campaign. Immediately I told her there had been
an explosion downtown and hung up—not
knowing then that the project we were discuss-
ing would end up on hold indefinitely.

I ran outside and looked downtown. To the
east, the sky was full of dust and dense black

smoke. You couldn't see anything through it—that's how thick it was. It darkened the streets, covering at least a square block.

Firefighters from Fire Station No. 1, right next door, and other fire department administrative staff from our building poured out to see what had happened. No one waited for the alarm that we all knew was coming. Instinct kicked in immediately. We scrambled to our vehicles and headed east down Fifth Street.

As my car topped the hill at Fifth and Walker, I was stunned to see the chaos in front of me. Smoke was pouring out from behind the Oklahoma Water Resources Building two blocks ahead at Fifth and Harvey. My first thought was that a plane had crashed. It never occurred to me that anybody would intentionally set out to cause this kind of destruction.

I pulled in across from the Regency Tower apartments. Out of the corner of my eye, I noticed quickly that all the windows had been blown out. The Water Resources Board offices also appeared to be heavily damaged. As I walked still closer, I discovered the actual source of the smoke—several cars burning. There was dense black smoke everywhere. A thick cloud of brown dust hung in the air. Bricks and debris filled the street. Everything was covered with dust and glass. In fact, the coating of broken glass made the entire scene glitter in the bright morning sun.

Dozens of dazed people wandered the streets,

many with blood streaming down their faces. People were running—some running for help while others were running *to* help. Paper rained from the sky.

Right away I got on the two-way departmental radio, as did everyone else, and started requesting help. The radio became immediately jumbled with all our conversations. Units were calling dispatch simultaneously. The crush of radio traffic jammed the airways. Oklahoma City Fire Chief Gary Marrs had arrived on the scene just ahead of me. He got on the radio and ordered silence from all the responding crews. Then he systematically started calling in dozens of units. Some crews from other fire stations were already rolling to the scene. Like ourselves, they had heard and felt the blast. They knew they would be needed.

It was instantly clear to all of us that we were in the middle of a major incident. But at that time we were still unaware of the full extent of the situation. Then the wind began to blow away the dust and smoke. Suddenly we got our first glimpse of the Alfred P. Murrah Federal Building—or should I say what was left of it!

For a moment I just stood there, stunned by what I was seeing. It was the most unbelievable sight I'd ever seen. The entire front of this huge building was gone. Though we knew at the time that this was the most significant incident we had ever faced, it would be days later before we would learn just how significant. This event would be named the worst terrorist act in American history.

My mind raced ahead, wondering about the fate of the hundreds of people inside. I had no idea what had caused the destruction. Frankly, it didn't matter. I knew we had what we refer to in our business as a mass casualty incident. We had a lot of very seriously injured people, and it was obvious that we would have some fatalities. The big question was: how many?

As I made my way to the front of the Federal Building (which faces north), I saw toys lying among the debris in the street. And it hit me. There was a day care center inside. My heart sank.

Then I turned to survey the entire scene. To the north I saw the Journal Record Building. The roof on one side of the building was gone. I looked toward the YMCA, across the street to the east, and saw tremendous damage there. I remembered the Y had a day care center, too. I could see kids already being brought out. Some were cut and bleeding—in pretty bad shape.

In fact, throughout the two-block area, there were dozens of people injured—adults and children. Some were walking on their own and others were being carried. Along with the toys scattered along the streets, furniture and other office materials had blown out of the Murrah Federal Building. There were cars that looked as if somebody had picked them up, crumpled them, and thrown them down on the pavement.

Bits of paper still fluttered from the sky. The entire block looked like something out of war-torn Bosnia.

Entering the Murrah Building from the northwest corner, I was met by a dark, heavy wall of dust and smoke. It was hard to breathe and the footing was unstable and treacherous.

Firefighters, volunteers, and police officers, first on the scene, were having to feel their way a step at a time—over broken concrete, loose wiring, exposed ductwork, twisted rebar, and broken glass in all shapes and sizes. Jumbled in the debris were desks, tables, chairs, file cabinets, personal effects—all the paraphernalia that made up the contents of the office building now destroyed and lying in pieces. Men and women made their way through wreckage, shouting out to people trapped inside the building. "Hey! We're here to help you. Call out to us if you can. . . ."

We were tortured by the victims we could see trapped in the debris. Many of them had been killed instantly by the blast. Where we could, we covered the bodies, but we had to leave them where they were for the time being. We had to keep focused on those we still might be able to save. For days we would work around the dead as we continued our search for the living. That constant presence of death weighed heavily on the rescuers as the search for survivors continued.

When we did find people alive, they were almost always entangled or trapped. The rescuers would kneel—or even lie down (if that was all space would allow)—next to survivors to provide comfort and reassurance until a crew could free them. In some cases medical teams treated the victims as we worked to get them loose. Other times, there was nothing any of us could do except be with that individual to the end. It was a dangerous and painful business for everyone involved.

Along with the darkness and difficult footing, rescuers had to contend with items falling on them from above—dust and bits of debris mostly—but sometimes pieces of conduit or ductwork or larger chunks of concrete.

We were still hours away from finding out how much structural damage had been done to the building. The fact that it continued to shift and crack caused great concern about the danger of additional collapse. But we had to keep our minds on the living victims and on getting to them quickly. Concerns for our own safety rarely entered our minds. Everyone working in the building was at risk of injury or death. But that's simply a part of the job we are trained to do. We all knew time was critical if we were to find and rescue living victims.

After a few minutes inside the building, I felt torn between what I wanted to do and what I needed to do. My gut reaction told me to stay in there and keep helping people. But the more disciplined side of me realized that there were sufficient numbers of people working in that role.

My job on the command staff was outside, helping to organize and coordinate the overall rescue effort. So that's where I headed.

At this point I saw an immediate need to help structure rescue efforts. We had a variety of people responding. Most were on-duty personnel. Others had just voluntarily rushed to the scene to help.

Considering the catastrophic nature of what had just happened, you might have expected people to be running from the area. Instead, people poured out of the buildings nearby, not to loot or gawk, but to help in whatever way was needed. These were regular everyday working Oklahomans. They pulled up in pickups and cars to help transport the wounded. They walked up to injured people on the streets and led them to a triage area to get medical treatment.

By now we had sounded a general alarm, which alerts every fire station in the city to respond at once. EMSA—our local ambulance service—had also called for every available unit to converge on the scene. Oklahoma City Police, County Sheriff's Deputies, and State Troopers turned out in full force within minutes. Some worked inside the building with us, while others cleared routes to all the nearby hospitals and worked to secure a perimeter around the damaged buildings. Ultimately, more than five hundred people would be treated at area hospitals on Wednesday—all but fifty-eight were released that same day.

A couple of blocks away, we gathered the leaders from each agency responding to the emergency and set up a command post to ensure a fully coordinated operation. From that point on, if any of us needed anything, we just turned to our counterparts, asked for it, and it happened. We weren't dealing with people who had to say, "Well, I have to check with my boss," or "I have to check with somebody else." There was a decision maker on site who could make things happen, and that worked very, very well.

It wasn't an accident that our emergency management system functioned as well as it did. Responding to disasters was something we had actually practiced. Less than a year earlier, all our local agencies who would be called in any real-life crisis had spent a week together in training. At the Emergency Management Institute in Emmitsburg, Maryland, we learned how to react during simulated crisis operations. Fifty representatives from the police and fire departments, EMSA, the city's Public Works Department and Department of Airports, the Red Cross, Salvation Army, other volunteer agencies plus the utility companies worked together to complete successfully a rigorous course in disaster management.

As a result, when this real-life crisis crashed in on us, we were able to quickly and efficiently coordinate efforts to rescue, evaluate, triage, treat, and transport victims. Our plan also allowed the team to track survivors to the various hospitals so we could link them up with loved ones who were desperate for information. The police department posted officers at every hospital to act as liaisons. The Red Cross provided a telephone hotline for families to call for information, while both the Red Cross and the Salvation Army provided immediate assistance at the scene.

Radio communication continued to be challenging because of the system overload—too many callers on too few frequencies. We had been working for a year on a strategy to use cellular phones in case of disaster. Without waiting to be asked, two local cellular phone companies responded to the crisis, providing cell phones, mountains of extra batteries, and chargers to every member of the command staff.

Mayor Ron Norick and the staff at his office took the necessary steps to set up a system to seek input from survivors about who was there at the time of the explosion. This critical information would allow search and rescue teams to have a better handle on how many people might still be trapped inside and where they might be found. City Manager Don Bown directed all departments to make every resource they had available to us. The Public Works Department arrived at the site with crews and equipment. The Department of Airports brought in lighting, generators, and fencing.

Our fire department was also able to draw on a system of mutual aid that had been developed through years of working with other area chiefs. Within minutes of the blast, other metro-area fire departments were providing personnel for the search and rescue effort downtown. They also supplied additional staffing from their own departments for the various Oklahoma City stations where crews had been reassigned to the disaster. This meant we could continue responding to the other needs of our citizens. EMSA got support from other area ambulance services as well, ensuring the entire city was covered at all times.

One of the success stories of this disaster would turn out to be the planning our community had done—primarily to prepare for the threat Oklahomans are most accustomed to: tornadoes. But perhaps as important as being prepared were the personal friendships we'd developed with our counterparts. We all knew each other by our first names. A lot of trust had been built up over the years. There was a tremendous amount of personal credibility and mutual respect between the lead agencies. When we all came together to form a unified command that morning, it was an impressive thing to witness. There was calm communication and smooth coordination from the start. And keep in mind that the people who benefited from that were the survivors. Leaders were able to focus on using all their energies and every conceivable resource to rescue victims from the Murrah Building and surrounding areas.

I also have to give credit to the local media. Radio, television, and newspaper reporters were all on the scene within minutes. They cooperated fully with our request to move back and keep everybody away from the scene. They also proved to be a valuable resource in getting important information out to the public.

All three local television affiliates and several radio stations scrapped their network programming and commercials. They carried continuous coverage live from the scene around the clock. Through radio and TV support we were able to limit the traffic downtown, keep major thoroughfares open for emergency vehicles, and clear phone circuits for emergency calls only. In the early stages, we were sharing information back and forth with reporters. In fact, that's how I first learned that investigators believed a car bomb had caused the destruction.

Once we had our initial command post in place, I spent much of the next hour back at the Federal Building, where we now had three aerial ladder trucks in place, giving us routes to the upper floors. Most of the surviving workers and visitors on the lower floors had made their way out on their own. Others had been assisted by rescue workers or those who were not too badly injured themselves.

From the street everyone could see the frightened individuals who had approached the ragged edge of what was left of the front of the building. Some were helped to safety through the stairways that were miraculously still intact. Others had to be coached down ladder rigs by firefighters.

17

There were probably a hundred rescuers inside the building initially—firefighters, police officers, paramedics, state troopers, military personnel, sheriff's deputies—on nearly every floor, in all the places we could reach. Some places could be accessed only by burrowing under the rubble through tiny crawl spaces. Rescuers were frantically looking through the debris, calling out to victims, trying to find survivors. Unfortunately, most of what we were finding were bodies. I was with Chief Marrs in front of the building when we got our second terrible jolt of the morning—reports of another bomb.

Immediately, a flash of panic raced through our minds: if this disaster were indeed the result of a bomb, then filling the building with firefighters and police for a second explosion might be part of a well-orchestrated sinister plot. Given the structure's weakened condition, a subsequent blast could be more deadly than the first. I felt my gut get tight. We knew we had rescuers deep inside the building, and it was going to take time to get them out. We never lost concern about the safety of the surviving victims, but with a hundred rescuers now inside, this latest threat dramatically increased the chances for additional loss of life. So within minutes of the notification, we ordered everybody out.

The decision to pull our people was made quickly. In truth, there was no choice to make. The first rule for those responding to an emergency is not to become victims themselves. However, getting everyone to comply was not as simple as giving the order to vacate the premises.

First, we had the logistical problem of getting word to rescue workers. Then they had to work their way out of the debris and down from the upper floors. When the call came to evacuate, some of our people were working to extricate victims from the debris that trapped them. We learned later that some of those rescuers opted to stay with the injured and ride out the threat. We didn't reprimand any of them for their decision. We felt it was one of those few times in life where there wasn't a right or wrong choice. Whatever each rescuer personally chose to do given each specific situation was the right thing to do.

When the building was evacuated, rescue workers were forced to leave some people who were conscious but trapped. Leaving was extremely tough on everyone who was sent out of the building, but it was obviously far worse for the victims left inside. I don't think any of us can ever really understand how horrible that moment was. These defenseless people had already been through the trauma of the first explosion. They were injured, trapped in debris, and had only just been found. Now they were learning that the rescuer holding their hand had to leave because there might be another explosion coming. The rescuers who saw their faces caught glimpses of pure terror, and those expressions are something they will carry with them for the rest of their lives.

To this day I've never been quite sure what caused the alarm. I was told at the time that somebody found something in the basement that appeared to be a bomb. Given the condition of the building, we had to react quickly. From that point on, a system was developed to verify sightings before we would stop the rescue effort again. There were reports in the media of other bomb scares, but this incident was the only one that caused us to vacate the entire building. And fortunately, this incident didn't cause much of a delay.

We were out of the building for only twenty to twenty-five minutes. We used the time to regroup, refocus, and talk to the firefighters who had been inside. With their firsthand accounts, we identified spots where victims were located and other areas where victims had not been sighted. We also collected valuable input about the successes and problems encountered up to that point.

We used this time to set goals, discuss resources, and outline strategies. As much as we wanted it to be a very quick rescue, we sensed early on that it was going to take a long time, that even the victims we'd already found were going to require some difficult and dangerous extrication.

Just before we returned to the building, we received some terrible news. Rebecca Anderson, a nurse who had come to the scene to provide medical assistance without concern for her own safety, had collapsed after coming from the building. There was speculation that her head injury had been caused by falling debris inside. The report renewed our fears about the safety of the people working to find survivors. We made a conscious decision that when we returned to the building, only rescue personnel in protective clothing would be allowed back inside.

The minute we got the all-clear signal, our crews began heading back into the building. As we watched them fighting their way through the treacherous tangle of debris, we knew we were a long way from being all-clear.

2

Miracles Do Happen

ONCE WE GOT back into the building, our progress seemed painfully slow. . . .

It had been over two hours since the massive explosion had ripped the building and people's lives into pieces. Our vision was still hampered by the dust and debris. We were often forced to rely on our instincts and flashlights to find our way in confined spaces. Chunks of concrete rested precariously on one another, ready to crash down on us at any moment. In some areas the floor constantly shifted beneath our feet as a result of large cracks and the loss of key support beams.

Anxious rescuers inched their way back into position, constantly calling out for survivors in an attempt to pinpoint their locations. We hoped that there would be more victims who were alive—and waiting desperately for help to come.

When we did find someone alive, the situation often required extensive disentanglement from the debris.

Because of the interior conditions of the building and the massive size of the building itself, it was difficult to know where to go next. Often the building dictated to us what we could do. There were areas where we believed victims were located but which we physically couldn't reach. It was extremely frustrating to rescue workers to be at the mercy of so much that was beyond our control.

The rescue strategy we devised was simple. We made an initial pass through the more accessible portions of the structure, looking for victims who were alive and easy to remove from imminent danger. Moving through the floors, making our inspection, it was hard to believe that the Murrah Building had been a bustling nine-story structure just hours before.

Once we felt comfortable that we had found everyone in the exposed areas, small groups of rescue workers were deployed to specific locations on each floor to begin the slow, tedious work of removing the debris piece by piece. We were looking for a hand or an arm or a foot, anything that might signal where there was a remaining survivor trapped and needing our assistance.

We refused to let ourselves become overwhelmed by the task in front of us. Even before we had the state-of-the-art instruments that would come, before we had sophisticated listening devices, before we had fiber-optic cameras, our rescue workers toiled diligently against seemingly insurmountable odds.

Our teams combed the wreckage, unsure where people would be found. Every now and then the teams would call for a "quiet" in some isolated section. A company officer would silence everyone working that area. Radios would be turned down. Like dozens of times before, the team leader would cry out to anyone within earshot: "Hey, make a noise! We are police officers and firefighters. Where are you?" Everybody would pause and strain to hear a response. They would shift positions, placing their ears down next to the debris itself.

Then they would shout into the rubble at the top of their lungs, "Hey, we're here to help you! Call out to us ... *please*." It was almost as if rescue workers were trying to will the survivors to live.

Then silence again. More waiting. Everyone was praying in their own way that we would hear a sound, any sound. We longed to hear a whisper or a sob or a tapping on the concrete that surrounded us. We strained our senses, already heightened by our deep desire to find someone, anyone.

Occasionally it happened. We got a response. And when we did, emotion would spread like wildfire through the entire building. Unfortunately, it didn't happen as often as we hoped. But when it did, the victory was felt by all.

While firefighters toiled slowly inside, continuing the laborious task of tackling this mammoth disaster, we were not alone. The entire city was rising to the challenges created by the most horrendous act ever perpetrated against our city.

Hospitals had shifted into an emergency mode, preparing for the hundreds of people that came and many more that would never live long enough to make it through their doors. Medical professionals flooded into emergency rooms all across town, offering assistance. The triage team routed ambulances to nearby medical centers.

Citizens, yearning for some way to help, lined up to give blood, many of them waiting hours because of the long lines. Blood banks set up additional locations, trying to accept the generosity of our citizens, but the turnout quickly overwhelmed the volunteer resources available.

The police worked endlessly all day to keep passageways clear. They were on hand to protect against looting and theft—but none occurred. This was best illustrated at the nearby bank whose plate glass windows broke, leaving cash drawers fully exposed—but no one stole a dime!

Help was coming from so many sources, it's hard to name everyone involved. Jim Loftis, one of the original architects of the Alfred P. Murrah Building, showed up with building plans that aided our constant assessments. Though the structure had been severely damaged, there was a lot of insight to be gained from looking at the plans. I guess you could compare their use in this case with an X ray of the human body. A doctor knows what specific functions each part of the human anatomy performs in a healthy individual. They use the X ray to see the differences and to make decisions about how to correct problems. We did the same thing with the building plans we were given.

Structural engineers were on site, helping to examine the ruins from a different point of view. It was their job to tell us what needed to be done to brace the shifting pillars that were making the inside of the building so unsafe. They viewed the layout, floor by floor, and made specific recommendations about using bracing and other support materials. They played a key role in helping us determine where there was the greatest possibility of survivors. Time and again they helped us discuss how we were going to remove certain parts of the building to reach new areas. At the outset, structural engineers estimated that we had three hundred tons of debris to get through.

Vital assistance came from other nontraditional sources as well. Among other items, the utility companies provided some ultrasensitive listening equipment. Southwestern Bell Telephone Company helped in so many ways, it would be impossible to state them all. Local construction companies provided equipment and workers.

Every step of the way was perilous. Power saws

were used to cut through concrete and twisted rebar, creating passageways to get us to areas where survivors might still remain. Each time we cut one place, we had to brace another. Each time we removed debris from an area, we had to reinforce the part of the building that was left. The entire experience was like working inside a huge Tinkertoy set. If we pulled the wrong piece out, who knew what might come tumbling down? The fear of further complicating the current nightmare demanded that we make well-reasoned decisions—every time.

That first afternoon, rescuers brought medical personnel into incredibly tight quarters to amputate the leg of a young woman. They had been working to free her since late morning. After much discussion, it was determined that if we attempted to cut through the concrete that pinned her, the result would probably be fatal. The chance was great that the entire section would collapse on her—and on the rescue personnel working to free her. We had fought too hard to find her and to keep her alive to lose her now. Fortunately, with good medical assistance and by the grace of God, we were successful in finally removing her and getting her to a local hospital for the care she needed.

The day care center was never far from anyone's mind. The fact that there were children to find kept everyone on edge. I'll never forget when I saw the playground area on the south side of the building. It had been set up as the temporary morgue. In many ways, it was the ideal place. For the children's protection, it had been purposely tucked away in an inconspicuous place. It was out of the view of the general public and its fencing and gate meant that the area had controlled and limited access. It was painfully ironic that this spot, where the children safely played, became the temporary resting place for those who were a testimony to the innocence we lost that day.

The number one question I was asked the first day, and in the days that followed, was about the children. The public was grieving for these children who had been robbed of their entire lives.

But the next most asked question, of course, was about the current death count. We were all highly aware that many more adults than children would have lost their lives by the time the rubble was cleared, and everyone was impatient to know how much grief the community would be forced to bear.

In determining the numbers we would release to the public, we were very careful. Above all, we wanted to avoid compounding the situation with unjustified numbers. Though we knew about how many people worked in the building, we had no idea exactly how many were in their offices at the time of the blast. It was also virtually impossible to guess how many citizens were in the building to do business that morning at nine o'clock.

We made a conscious effort to be accurate in

the numbers we released. In the aftermath of this tragedy, with so many rescue workers moving around in the disaster area, it would have been easy to double- and triple-count people. After careful planning, we determined that the official count of the deceased would be based on the actual number of bodies turned over to the medical examiner.

At the same time, we also established a list of missing persons from several sources. Information was organized, as we discussed earlier, by Mayor Norick's office. Agency heads and workers who survived provided information about the federal employees likely to have been in the building at the time of the blast. The medical examiner's office provided input. Citizens from the community who suspected that their family members or neighbors might have been in the building that morning also added names to the list.

Clearly, whenever a survivor was pulled from the wreckage or a body was extracted, adjustments were made to the count. As an individual was identified by the staff at the medical examiner's office, we would make a revision. In some cases, people who were initially thought to be in the building were found alive other places. When these variables would periodically change the number of persons reported missing, new numbers would be issued.

We had immediately assigned district chiefs to survey the surrounding buildings with their crews to assess the damage. Some of the hardest hit were just across the street. The Journal Record Building had a portion of its roof blown off, and the windows were gone. With only a parking lot between this stately old structure and the truck that housed the bomb, nothing stood in the way of mass destruction. Many people working in the building received injuries of all kinds. Double-paned windows blew in on them. As if that weren't enough, ceiling tiles, wallboard, and lighting fixtures came tumbling down on them, too.

The parking lot next to the Journal Record Building had been full of burning cars when we'd arrived earlier that morning. Though we had put the fires out, we went back later in the day to review the damage. Even closer to ground zero was the Athenian Building, which partially shielded the Oklahoma Water Resources Building. Bearing the brunt of the blast on the north side of the street, the Athenian Building was pretty much demolished.

The YMCA across the street, the ABC Cab Company, the First United Methodist Church, St. Joseph's Cathedral, the C. R. Anthony corporate headquarters, and virtually every building for blocks was affected. Giant plate glass windows in high-rise office towers and other businesses were no match for the powerful explosives in this bomb. Glass was everywhere: on the floors, desks, sidewalks, in people's hair, and on their clothes. Pictures and certificates blew off walls.

Lighting fixtures plummeted. Though we couldn't place a value on the losses that first day, we knew that lives had been turned upside down and businesses had been destroyed.

Days later Public Works Director/City Engineer Paul Brum would tell us that damage costs would be in the millions. The bomb driven into downtown Oklahoma City left no surprise about what nearly five thousand pounds of explosives will do. It will change things forever.

Later that night, the first of eleven Federal Emergency Management Agency/Urban Search And Rescue (FEMA/USAR) teams arrived from Phoenix, Arizona. They began working just after midnight to help us move debris in our continued attempts to locate survivors. As we carried piles out of the building, federal authorities took custody of them, sifting through every piece for even the smallest shred of evidence—anything that might provide a clue to who had committed this heinous crime. We were proud of the professionalism our local authorities exhibited. We also appreciated guidance from one of the lead federal agents, who had investigated the World Trade Center bombing.

Throughout the first day, we combined modern equipment with other rescue methods that are as old as the human race. We utilized highly trained dogs, first from the Oklahoma City Police Department's canine units, and then later search and rescue dogs arrived with the FEMA/USAR teams. The dogs made a lot of hits as they worked their way through the building, saving us valuable time from the beginning.

Even these animals could not escape the human kindness that our community was pouring out on everyone involved in the rescue effort. When one of the local reporters did a story about the dogs' bleeding paws, injured from climbing through the rubble, the public responded. In a follow-up live shot, the reporter asked for donations of dog boots to protect the animals' paws from broken glass and scraps of sharp metal. The site was a dangerous place and these animals were walking through the building essentially barefoot. Within hours, scores of dog booties had been donated. In the end, the dogs couldn't wear the boots because the trainers explained that they needed their claws to climb, but the story is yet another demonstration of the generosity shown by Oklahomans, whatever the need appeared to be at the time.

The search and rescue dogs never gave up. They put their hearts into their job. Just like our human workers, trainers had to find ways to keep their four-legged partners' morale high. Sometimes after long periods of searching, rescue workers would hide in the wreckage and the dogs would be sent in to search. Finding someone alive boosted their spirits, just as it did ours. We were all longing for the real thing.

That's why excitement raced through the building so quickly when, at 9:15 P.M., firefighters found a survivor, Brandy Liggons. It had been twelve long hours since the bomb exploded, seven hours since workers had removed the previous survivor, Dana Bradley. Hope was renewed in the heart of every person in America.

Amazingly enough, Brandy was found less than fifteen feet south and five feet east of where we had located Dana earlier that morning. However, tons of rubble separated them. Brandy's condition prevented her from calling out, so we never heard a sound from the fifteen-year-old girl who had been in the building getting her social security card. Making their way through debris in the building late that night, rescuers realized Brandy was alive when they shone their flashlights on her and she opened her eyes.

It took forty-five minutes to free her, and shortly before ten P.M. she was safely transported to an ambulance and sent to a nearby hospital. At the time we had no idea that Brandy would be the last survivor we would find in the Murrah Building. In fact, at least for that night, the thought never crossed our minds. We were emotionally recharged, and the memory of Brandy's rescue would carry us far into the days ahead.

3

The Pit, the Pancake, and the Cave

IN BROAD DAYLIGHT, what remained of the Alfred P. Murrah Federal Building was one of the most intimidating sights anyone in our state had ever seen. People came from the far corners of Oklahoma to see it for themselves and, when they arrived, they would stand and stare in disbelief.

But nighttime added an even worse dimension to the place. The front side stood out from the blackness, bathed in floodlights. It was as bright as broad daylight on Fifth Street, and that's no exaggeration. The giant lights towered over dump trucks now on the scene.

Inside was another story. There were obviously many places that were so hidden away that the light couldn't shine. Dangling debris blocked much of the light trying to find its way into the building, creating frightening shadows. In some areas, like the area we designated "the cave," we had been using flashlights during the daylight hours, so you can imagine how dark it became in those places when the sun finally set that first night.

Interior lights were set up throughout the building for the safety of rescuers. Stark brightness alternated with deep shadows. As we rounded corners, larger-than-life figures seemed to dance along the broken sections of the walls.

It was an eerie feeling . . . as we walked from one section to another. The lighting conditions changed our perspective of the building. That, coupled with the full range of sounds that became a normal part of our lives for sixteen days, was an indescribable experience. Dangling light fixtures and shredded conduit flapped in the Oklahoma wind that whistled through the ruins of the building. It was impossible to shut out the sound of rattling remnants of rebar and falling debris.

The building itself was overpowering. What many people didn't take into account when they saw pictures on television is that those shots were taken from a vantage point several blocks away from the site. When you stood near the crater resulting from the bomb and looked up, the ruins were like a mountain looming in front of you. The building was so massive that it had occupied its own city block the night before. Now a very large portion of it was totally gone. The remains, thick concrete slabs and granite chunks, were randomly lying about. It looked like someone had picked up a major avalanche in the Rocky Mountains and dropped it here in the Heartland.

Working inside a building left with so little structural integrity, rescue workers faced new challenges each hour, but we were motivated by our memories of successful rescues from that first day. The experience of those victories— freeing a survivor, hearing a feeble cry for help, removing rubble and having a hand reach out to you—all these things kept us going.

Liberating yet another survivor—that was our ongoing hope. We would shift a piece of debris. We would move a key piece of rubble. The dogs would make a hit. The cameras would pick up something. We were constantly working to find another hard-earned victory.

As if the building weren't daunting enough, the weather also had to take its shot at us. Several times, storm clouds filled the skies, creating new challenges for all of us. As someone in the media suggested, it was as if the sky were crying, too, over the needless destruction and despair that so many felt.

Stiff winds with gusts of up to forty mph and the driving rain forced us briefly to stop working on occasion. Anytime there was lightning we had to shut down the cranes—which limited our speed and progress. As the days went on, the temperature dropped and it was unseasonably cool. All these factors increased the burden on rescue workers to move quickly to find and recover victims. I guess Will Rogers was right when he used to say, "If you don't like the weather in Oklahoma, just wait a little while—'cause it will change." And throughout the rescue effort, it did.

Over the sixteen-day operation, we used special terminology to describe different areas of the building where rescuers were searching for victims. The nickname most often used by rescuers was "the pit." Certainly when we began working to find survivors, the word bore absolutely no resemblance to the place, because that part of the building was entirely filled with debris. The section was located in the center of the building, where debris from the second and third floors had been dumped on the first floor. We hoped that there was a chance that a survivor from higher up may have been swept with other falling debris into this area.

We worked diligently, taking out load after load of rubble, hoping to uncover someone alive. We unearthed personal mementos, office supplies, and children's toys as we moved through the broken pieces of concrete. Everything was completely jumbled up. Rescuers would find a child's shoe, then a family photo, then a pile of checks. Although we carried away tons of wreckage, sadly we were unable to find any additional survivors as we completed our rescue activities in the pit.

Most people heard the term "pancake," for we talked about it every day. The pancake was created when a large portion of the building's entire nine floors crashed down, resting in a pile between twenty and thirty feet high. This amount of compression meant that these collapsed floors had essentially become a solid mass of concrete. Stacked on top of one another, they picked up the nickname "pancake."

Like most areas of the building, we sifted through much of the pancake by hand. We started with the roof and the ninth floor and worked our way down. Construction workers helped us break the floors up into more manageable pieces. Cables were wrapped around the larger sections and cranes would lift them out of our way. Each time we removed the flooring materials, it exposed another group of offices that we could carefully search through.

Sometimes we were able to determine the office area where we were working by letterhead or other items we found. Glass was everywhere we worked, ready to wound rescuers if they weren't careful. There were other items to be found that cut just as deeply—into our hearts. Handwritten memos being penned at the time of the blast, never to be finished or read. Family photographs and crumpled certificates once proudly displayed. The tattered Stars and Stripes that were ripped to shreds by flying debris. A toy fire truck that was possibly the dream of one young boy in the day care center. The sinking feeling we felt as we moved some rubble to uncover an arm, then the torso, and finally, a lifeless body.

Rescue workers also spoke about "the cave" when they described where they were performing search responsibilities. The Federal Building was constructed with a split-level ground floor. Access to Fifth Street from one side and Fourth Street from another created a pocket where we felt that chances were good that we would find survivors. And in fact the cave is where we found the last two survivors.

Those who found their way into the cave said that it was like a throwback to the old mining days. We shored up the section with timbers to create a passageway barely wide enough for two workers to pass. Rescuers crawled on their hands and knees, using flashlights fastened to their helmets to see what lay ahead. An incredible amount of material filled pathways to the sheltered spots where the structural engineers suggested that safe havens might occur.

Minutes extended into hours. Hours stretched into days. Frankly, the days blurred together as time went on. We were continuing our systematic search, pressing our bodies through cracks and crevices to reach isolated areas.

One of the most frustrating parts of the entire operation was an exceptionally large piece of concrete—rescuers dubbed it "the mother slab." This huge section of the ninth floor roof was hanging high and deep inside the building, dangling by rebar over the area below. The impact of the blast had not broken it completely loose, and it was left to create an incredibly dangerous situation for workers and to delay work in areas we were eager to search.

Structural engineers gave us differing opinions about its stability. Some said the mother slab would definitely fall. Others thought it was secure where it was—that it would have already fallen if it were going to. Until everyone could reach a consensus, we had to label the area underneath it as one of the primary no-go zones to ensure the safety of our firefighters.

The slab, now hanging vertically, extended from the ninth floor all the way down to the seventh floor. This created even greater concern because of the momentum it would build before crashing onto the rubble far below. Furthermore, one engineer voiced the opinion that if the mother slab did drop, it wouldn't fall straight; instead, it would angle back toward the central supports of the building.

Because of the safety risk this dangerous piece posed for rescuers, we never took any chances about what it might do. We constantly monitored its stability by an around-the-clock watch.

Our concerns were well founded. When attempts were made to clean some accumulated debris from the mother slab, it rotated and worked itself into an even more precarious position.

We considered every alternative we could think of to deal with the problem. Lowering it? That could be a bad idea. If we lost control of it, the slab could bring down part of the building. Try to cut it up somehow? Equally dangerous. Finally we made the only decision we felt was an option: to leave it where it was but to secure it to the building as best we could. This answer would still require keeping an eye on the problem even after the slab was anchored in place.

At all times we took the advice of our structural engineers. We began to affectionately refer to them as our guardian angels. If something looked dangerous in the area we were working, they'd pull firefighters back while they investigated. Because the building was severely traumatized, at times it would crack or shift, requiring additional reinforcement be added to the support beams. In fact, the structural specialist monitoring the building noted that it had shifted over two feet from the time he began taking measurements until we finished our work.

We never really shifted from a search and rescue mode into an exclusive recovery phase until very late in the operations, but that's a technicality that doesn't hold much distinction anyway, as the same essential steps have to be completed for both survivors and victims. That was particularly true in this case, where it was so important to extract bodies in the best condition possible so they could be identified.

We were still hopeful through the first week that we would find survivors, based on what had happened in building collapses in other parts of the world. In the Mexico City earthquake, there were babies found in a hospital ward almost a week following the incident. In California, rescue workers had found survivors three and four days after the earthquake. So we certainly had no intention of giving up hope. As time went on, our minds may have realized that the clock was working against us, but our faith kept us going.

Even after we passed the seven-day point, we still didn't give up hope despite the fact that we were beginning to be less optimistic. We knew with certainty that the clock and weather were working against us. We realized that the chance of finding another survivor was getting slim—but we kept believing.

While we hadn't given up hope, eventually we did redirect some of our workforce to recover the expired victims we had found in the days before. That explains why the fatality count grew slowly at first and then escalated. There was also a significant jump in the fatality count as we entered those parts of the structure closer to ground zero.

There were several reasons we hadn't gone right into the areas where we suspected there were multiple fatalities. The primary one was the high degree of damage to the structure in those locations, specifically those areas that took the full force of the blast: the social security office on the first floor, America's Kids Day Care Center on the second floor, and the Federal Employees Credit Union on the third floor.

We suspected that the people in those areas were blown from the front of the building toward the back before the upper floors came smashing down. It was hard to know the answer for sure because these were the same areas that were so deeply buried by the heavy burden of the floors above. To find the answers people were waiting to hear, we had to dig slowly and systematically until we reached the bottom.

In the end, the search yielded generalized patterns. Rescue workers did find that many of the people on the lower three floors were blown back into the building by the blast. They were the toughest to reach because they were the most deeply buried. Victims on the fourth through the ninth floors, where the building gave way, dropped nearly straight to the ground.

As we approached the final day of the rescue and recovery operation, the men and women who had already worked for fifteen days inside the Federal Building pressed on. It had been emotional for us from day one, but our feelings grew more intense as we realized the end of the recovery effort was near.

4

The Search Ends,
The Healing Begins

By Thursday, May 4, all the out-of-state rescue crews who had come to Oklahoma in the days after the explosion had packed up and returned home. This meant those left to finish the search were those of us who had started it: Oklahoma City firefighters.

A hardy group of individuals, most rescuers working at the site had no idea what day it was or how many days they had been sorting through the chaos the bomb had left behind. In fact, it was almost as if in some ways time had stopped for the past fifteen days. We had now removed nearly 450 tons of debris one layer at a time. Having started at the top, working down, as well as from the front, working back, it looked as if the search would finally end. Where there had been piles of rubble, everything was gone.

Throughout the search and rescue effort, the

firefighters inside the building never lost their focus. This nightmare had consumed the men and women who felt a deep commitment to finish the task in front of them for the sake of the victims' families. Even when individuals were forced to take some time off, for most it gave them little relief. Our hearts and thoughts stayed in the building regardless of where we were.

Crews had worked hard throughout the search but never as hard as in those last twenty-four hours. Everyone knew that we planned for the Oklahoma City firefighters to leave the Alfred P. Murrah Federal Building for the last time together at the end of the day. That morning I explained to the media we were reaching the south wall of the structure's gutted portion. I told them we felt it was possible that we could find the remaining victims there before day's end. It was the only place left to search.

There was an urgency about the search and recovery effort all that day. We had worked at maximum capacity for days. Surprisingly, we drew additional energy out of ourselves that we didn't know existed because we were so driven to provide some peace, some closure, to the operation. Frankly, the idea that we might have to leave before finishing the job—recovering every victim—weighed heavily on every firefighter there.

The recovery of eleven adult victims and three infants by late evening pushed the blast's death toll to 164, but two people were still missing.

Considering the condition of the building, being able to recover all but two people would be, in the community's eyes, a major accomplishment. For us—well, it was tough to not focus on the two people we hadn't yet been able to recover for their families.

As a team, we agreed there was going to be no way to search the last debris pile—which rested against the most severely damaged and unstable column in the building. Structural engineers told us that moving the rubble from that spot could bring the column and some of the remaining structure crashing down on rescuers. By eleven-fifty that night, we'd searched everything but that last pile—and still had not found the two missing people. The time had finally come when we had to admit we'd done everything humanly possible and that the building would allow us to do.

I was standing next to Chief Marrs when he made the call to end the operation. With emotion in his voice he said, "That's it. We can't go any further." Even though there was a sense of relief that this sixteen-day ordeal was finally over, it was a particularly somber moment.

We found our way to the special memorial that our rescue workers had created so that we would have a private spot to pay our respects at the scene. This was our own place filled with things we'd found, made, or been given. There was a slab painted GOD BLESS THE CHILDREN AND THE INNOCENT. An American flag hung among flowers, teddy bears, a baby's pacifier, poems, personal notes. Each of the FEMA/USAR teams had gathered at the memorial one last time before returning back home. Now it was our turn.

It was a very small group. Chief Marrs, the fire department's chaplain, Ted Wilson, and I got up on an elevated area. We all took our helmets off. Chief Marrs expressed his thanks and gratitude to all the rescue workers and confirmed how much he appreciated their dedication, their sincerity, their positive attitude through this tragedy. He told the firefighters how proud he was to be their chief, then he turned to me and asked if I had any comments I wanted to make.

It was the strangest thing. I'm the guy who made comments to everyone about the incident all along the way, and suddenly I was speechless. There was nothing I could think of to say.

Chaplain Ted said a few words, and we had a prayer, followed by a moment of silence. Then our group went through our critical stress defusing session which lasted about thirty minutes.

I had one last job to do. I still had to face what was probably the toughest moment in the entire incident for me personally—telling the media that we had ended the search. I walked slowly toward the media area, stopping to speak to the state troopers guarding the perimeter, delaying the inevitable. Ideas about what I would say were rolling through my head.

As I walked, I was still searching for the words to use in this final announcement from the search and rescue team. I was thinking about the

164 people we had removed from the building, about the two victims we hadn't found in the search, about the nurse who bravely gave her life—167 people the nation mourned. I was thinking about the firefighters I'd just left and the hundreds of rescuers and others who had also played a part in the operation. I was thinking about the families that had lost so much. I was thinking about the spirit and generosity of our community and how people all across this country had supported us while we tried to recover from the most violent terrorist act in our nation's history.

At twelve thirty-five A.M. I informed a very reverent and somber group of professional journalists that the ordeal was over. My words weren't eloquent, just short and to the point: "It's over." There simply wasn't anything else left to say.

Friday came and I thought back to my comment the night before. It wasn't that easy—the simple act of leaving the building did not mean that we had left the corner of Fifth and Robinson in downtown Oklahoma City behind. I know the men and women I work with and I'd come to know this community in a very personal way over the past two weeks. Clearly, today would be just the first step of many for those of us trying to return to our day-to-day routines.

There would be a lot of adjustments to be made. Rescuers had missed out on so much. I'd talked with media from all over the world, so I understood how significant these past two weeks had been for the country. Many of the people who performed the search and rescue operations inside the building were less prepared for the overwhelming appreciation of the community.

The teams who worked in the building had been so focused on their task that they didn't have a chance to follow the story of what had happened, as did the rest of the country. They didn't understand that many people would treat them differently now—that children would grab them by the arm and call them heroes. The uniform has always carried a certain respect, but this outpouring of appreciation had become more than that. People had lived this tragedy through us and they respected the job we did. Somehow—and not at our initiative—this had taken on a whole new dimension.

That afternoon, rescuers gathered with family and friends at the base of the building to pray and remember the victims in a memorial service. Thousands of people showed up to pay their respects and to grieve with one another. There were lots of tears and a small sense of relief. For many it was the first chance they'd had to publicly deal with the emotion of what they'd been doing the past sixteen days.

Oklahoma's First Lady, Cathy Keating, made sure that each of us was given a rose when we arrived, to keep or to use as a way to pay our respects. Most of us chose to add ours to the memorial we'd been maintaining in front of the building. I stood and watched while rescuers, often hand in hand with family members, placed their flowers among the mementos that we'd left there, pausing now for a moment to say goodbye.

One of our firefighters had another idea about what to do with his rose. In a private moment, when no one was around, he walked to the place in the building where we believe the unrecovered victims will be found. Tossing his rose on the remaining rubble, he offered a personal promise: "When the building comes down, I'll be back to get you."

As rescuers left, hundreds of citizens standing outside the area shouted their thanks and applauded to show their appreciation. Again, many rescuers had tears running down their faces from the reminder that the goodness in people had carried us through this nightmare.

On Saturday, thousands of survivors and relatives of victims were given the opportunity to visit the site at a private time planned by the Oklahoma City Police Department. Many had not had the chance to go to the building yet, and they wanted the experience to help them with their closure. Police Chief Sam Gonzales, Captain Bill Citty, and Sergeant Bill Martin worked very hard putting everything together—and they did an outstanding job.

My three-year-old daughter, Jill, went with me that morning. Between my wife Jenifer's job as a local TV news anchor and my responsibilities on the command staff, Jill was aware that some bad men had blown up a building and we were working to help the people who were hurt. She wanted to go with me when I left the house Saturday, and I wanted to take her.

Again, Oklahoma's First Lady made sure everyone was provided with a rose. When Jill saw the teddy bears at the rescuers' memorial, she asked if she could put our rose there with them. I put Jill down as she smiled at the military and police honor guard who were watching our "treasures." She walked over as close as she could get, bent over, put the rose down, and came back to be picked up by me once more. I gave her a big hug and a kiss. It was a very special moment. It probably meant more to me than it did to her because of her age, but it's a memory I'll never forget as long as I live.

There were other special guests there, but one group deserves particular acknowledgment. Earlier that day, thanks to the hard work of John Boyle of the Dearborn Police Department, seventy police officers from twenty-seven agencies arrived from Michigan in a motorcade of squad cars. They had driven straight through from Lansing to present Oklahomans with a gift of $70,000 for the relief effort. When the caravan reached the Oklahoma border around midnight, the Oklahoma Highway Patrol was waiting to escort them the final hundred miles.

The people of Michigan, throughout the entire incident, had demonstrated their pain at being associated with this tragedy because of the investigation. This group of officers wanted to do something significant to replace that negative tie with a more positive connection.

Typical of the graciousness and appreciation that Governor Keating demonstrated from day one, he asked that a representative from the Michigan delegation join the honor guard at the site. The officers were deeply moved by the gesture, saying they came to show support to the city and they ended up being humbled by the support that the people of Oklahoma showed them. Like many others, they experienced the heart and the soul of these folks we proudly call "Okies."

It was a difficult time for all of us as the families of victims came face-to-face with the battered building that was a symbol of all they had lost. They stood very still and most were very quiet as they stared in disbelief at the devastation. You could see them pointing at the gaping wreckage, talking about where their loved ones had worked. Tears found their way to many faces that day. No one was immune to the impact of the emotion that charged the air.

As they were leaving, one of the family members asked if she could have a piece of the building. Police had restricted access behind barricades about forty feet from the building to protect visitors from any debris that might fall. But those of us there to help were eager to do anything to provide these wonderful people with even a moment's relief. Police Chief Sam Gonzales, Fire Chief Gary Marrs, and I found some of the yellow plastic buckets we had used to remove material from the site and filled them with chunks of concrete and debris. As family members and survivors reached into the buckets and held a piece in their hands, I couldn't help but think that it was so little to offer people who deserve so much more.

5

Oklahoma's Children = America's Kids

THE EXPLOSION CAME at 9:02 in the morning, and it was apparently timed to catch people just settling down to work. But what tested the limits of grief from the first day was the day care center, one floor up, where most of the nineteen children died.

The name of the day care center? America's Kids, and that is certainly what these innocent young victims were to become over the days that followed.

Working in the day care area was extremely tough for all of the rescuers. Knowing that at any moment you could turn over a piece of concrete or steel and find the body of a small child—well, the thought of it broke our hearts. The reality was even worse.

Even so, the rescue workers tried to get to the day care center immediately. Most of it was buried beneath tons of concrete, but there was a small area that escaped destruction. Firefighters and police officers dug through the debris they could reach, searching for a small hand that would reach out to them for help. They could hear the cries of surviving children—cries that will ring in their ears for the rest of their lives.

A few children were found alive, and our hearts soared each time one was lifted from the destruction. As they were passed from person to person, each rescuer held the children tight, trying to assure them that they were safe in spite of the fact that their world had just been blown apart.

Throughout the operation we would focus first on our search for the living, but in this small area of the day care area, this corner that had survived total collapse, exceptions were made. Firefighters would pick up the lifeless bodies of children and cradle them close. They couldn't bear to look down at the children in their arms, but they would hug them tight ... wanting to pass some of their life into the little ones. They wanted so desperately to do something that would save these children's lives. But in the end there was nothing that could be done for all but a few.

The decision was made to remove all the children's bodies as we discovered them. When it was time to turn and pass a child to someone else in the human chain, the line of rescue workers taking children out of the building, it was in-

credibly difficult. Firefighters in the day care area
didn't want to let go of the children. They didn't
want to give up in this fight against death and destruction. Doing that was like having someone
drive a stake through their own hearts. A part of
all of us died with each lifeless child found entangled in the rubble that day—and in the days
that followed.

Outside the building, the interaction with children was heartbreaking, but much more laced
with a sense of hope. There were injured children from the YMCA Day Care Center lined up
and down the street, but at least they were alive.
Many were frightened and bleeding, and volunteers were working feverishly to calm their spirits
as the world around them was spinning fast. Parents were rushing to the scene and ambulances
were preparing to take those needing immediate
medical attention to nearby hospitals.

Many of the children had stuffed animals they
were clutching, trying to squeeze a sense of security out of the madness that surrounded them.
Some of the stuffed toys had come out of the
building with the children, but many were
brought to the scene by police officers or state
troopers who had them in their cars to use in
traumatic situations. And this certainly was such
a time.

As I walked through the area, talking with
those who had carried the children to safety, I
noticed that there was one little child who didn't
have a toy to hold. I knelt down in front of him,

taking off my helmet and placing it in his lap. That frightened little boy wrapped his arms around it and held it close. As I talked with him, he never loosened his grip, and for a moment I thought I might never get my headgear back. That would have been fine with me, but it seemed like the little fellow deserved more comfort than a hard piece of plastic could provide. An observant police officer saw this child's need and brought him a new, clean stuffed animal. He quickly gave up the battered helmet for the softer alternative and I certainly understood why. As for me, that helmet took on a new value that day. It became something I'll never ever part with.

Parents were still frantically flooding into the area. I didn't personally notice any of them going into the building to try to find their children, but that feat would not have been an easy one to accomplish. The state of the building after the blast would have deterred most people, as the area where they had dropped off their children was completely gone. Police officers worked quickly to restrict access to the premises because it was clearly unsafe for anyone not wearing protective clothing.

Early on at the command post two men walked up to me, directed my way by other firefighters. They were looking for news about their children. My heart just about stopped. My mind was racing, wondering what in the world I would tell these parents. I had just come out of the building. I knew the extent of the devastation, especially to the day care area. I'd talked to firefighters about what they had just been going through trying to remove children, both dead and alive.

I still hadn't said anything to the two men in front of me, fighting the big lump in my throat, when one of them asked if they could go to the building. "No, sir," I said. "The premises are entirely too dangerous. If you will just step over by the curb across the street, we'll be with you in a minute."

As I turned away, I was struggling inside myself about what to do. I was trying to stay focused, but I kept thinking, "What if I were the one looking for information? What if Jill had been inside that building?" I was glad that in addition to being a firefighter, I was also the father of a three-year-old, because that caused me to rethink what had just happened.

I walked across the street and approached those two fathers, terror gripping their faces and their hearts. I tried to push my own grief aside to help them, asking that they try to stay as calm as possible until they received confirmed information. I told them that we were in the process of setting up a place where they would be able to learn exactly what was happening with the search in the day care area.

David Hackett, of the American Red Cross, had given me a phone number that would be activated in fifteen minutes. I'd written the number on a card for the two fathers. Just having something, anything to hold in their hands, seemed to help. I had to keep fighting the frustration inside me—having nothing more to give these two men than a phone number and a minute of kindness.

There were other times I was asked about the children, by parents and by those who were on the scene offering their assistance. It wasn't surprising, as the people downtown aren't any different from the rest of the world. We were all shaken, baffled, and confused by the reality that someone could do something like this to innocent, unsuspecting people—especially to children.

There were lots of tears in those first few hours—for those who were lost, for those who had lost someone, for those who were patiently waiting while we searched through the debris of concrete and steel for any sign of human life and a reason to hope.

Each time someone would ask me to tell them what was happening in the day care area, I hardly knew what to say. I saw people standing in front of me numb and in shock, struggling with the reality of this awful disaster. You could see in their faces that they were searching for someone to tell them that this was all a bad dream and everything would be all right. Their eyes were pleading with me to tell them that their child had been spared. I couldn't do it. Frankly, I knew what the odds were, but I didn't know about their child specifically. I hoped that every parent was the parent of one of the few children we had found alive in that first hour.

Following a brief meeting in the command post, a police officer called me over to talk with three young ladies, two sitting on the ground, one with her arm around the other. He said to me, "Jon, these are some people who need information. One is the mother of a child who was in the Federal Building's day care center at the time of the blast. They've been to the front of the building and seen the devastation. They've seen some of the kids brought out who were injured or killed inside. They really need to talk with someone."

So I took off my helmet and knelt down. I'll never forget that moment when that mother looked me right in the eye, tears streaming down her face. She asked, "Where's my baby?" It was a simple question. But there was no simple answer.

I wanted to be sensitive and I knew the best thing for her at that time was to contact the Red Cross. They had the best information available to families—along with support personnel to help parents deal with the news, whatever it was.

There was no dodging the issue with this mother. This wasn't like talking to people who were being detained at the perimeters. This woman knew. She had seen the nightmare up close. She knew the violence that had blown through that building almost as well as I did. She had seen that there was no day care center left. I don't remember another moment during the entire operation when I had a more helpless feeling in my gut. Even if I had wanted to be the one to tell her what had happened to her child, I couldn't. I didn't know anything. We hadn't been given names to go with the faces of the children who were brought out—injured or dead.

There was nothing I could do but kneel there and spend some time with them. After we talked for a while, she stood up and gave me a hug, and the gesture brought tears to my eyes. Her compassion in the midst of her own personal tragedy was almost more than I could bear. She headed to the Red Cross area and I returned to the site. I never saw her again.

Later the first day, word spread through the building that there was a bomb threat at nearby Children's Hospital, where many of the young victims had been transported. We immediately sent a fire response team over there, but thankfully we had enough people activated so that it didn't slow the rescue and recovery efforts. In fact, if anything, the hospital bomb threat helped us accelerate our pace. To think that someone would put kids hurt by this bomb and now in intensive care through anything else—well, it was absolutely cruel and heartless. Nothing short of pathetic. More than one of us stopped and offered a prayer different from the one that had been flowing from our hearts since early that morning. This time we prayed that police would find the sick people who were playing with the lives of these defenseless kids.

As the days turned into weeks, we never had the buried day care center far from our thoughts. Early on, rescue leaders told workers to picture what it would be like to find a child alive—and it was one of the things that kept us going. At the same time, that part of the building's rubble also scared us the most. We knew that it would take hundreds of hours to get there and what we would find when we arrived would no doubt be bad beyond description.

The best news of the operation was when we learned from Melva Noakes, the director of the America's Kids Day Care Center, that the number of missing children was far less than we had first feared. There were fewer children enrolled in the program than we had originally been told by people making "best-guess" projections. The news lifted some of the weight of what we felt. Not that our grief for those who had been murdered in this blast and avalanche of debris was diminished, but there was a huge sense of relief that there would be less to face when we finally arrived at the day care.

Arrive at the day care. That's a phrase that meant something different to those of us working in the building than it meant to the people watching and waiting in front of their televisions every day. Reporters would ask me over and over, "When will you get to the day care center?" It wasn't until we were several days into the rescue effort that I realized that meant something different to most of them than it meant to us.

Because of the media location, reporters didn't have the three-dimensional view of the building that we did. It almost shocked me when I realized that in most people's minds they thought we were digging through the rubble and eventually we would reach an area, a door that if opened would put us in the day care center. That couldn't have been further from the truth.

The day care center was gone, crushed by the weight of the tons of concrete and steel that had crashed on top of it. When rescuers talked about "getting to the day care area" we meant that we would have successfully dug down to where it was. Frankly, after the first thirty minutes to an hour, there wasn't much of the day care we could reach, as most of it made up the lower levels of the pancake area out front. As I've mentioned before, conduit, wires, infrastructure of the building, plumbing, furniture—all these elements made it almost impossible to move.

It wasn't our intent to mislead anyone about the ultimate fate of those in the day care area, but in a way I'm glad that this misunderstanding happened. It meant that the rest of the world didn't have to suffer through the same agony that we did initially. There would be plenty of time for that when reality would force its way into their lives, too.

In the first few days after the blast, we told the press as exactly as possible when we would reach the area. Then the debris would shift, the weather would change, something would happen to slow us down. We were constantly being frustrated by structural challenges and other obstacles. Finally, when it became clear that it was nearly impossible to estimate our speed, we quit making projections. We'd simply report what we'd accomplished when we were finished. That seemed to work better for everyone involved and relieved some of the pressure we were putting on ourselves. The situation inside the building was pressure enough.

We constantly monitored the mental health of the rescuers working in the building, especially when they were in the day care area. If a crew was responsible for removing a child from the building, that ended their shift. They went straight to a stress management session. There are some situations too tough to ignore, and we felt that this was an experience that required immediate attention.

There were other children in the building. I remember one time in particular when we found a woman and a child who had died from the blast. When we found them, the woman was holding the child, so at least we knew that child had died in the arms of someone who loved him. As time went on, we received more information from the Mayor's office about people who were visiting the building and we were able to know when we were approaching an area where we would probably locate a child. It helped us prepare mentally, and that was good.

America's Kids. The name of a day care center that would capture the hearts and minds of America. But the America's Kids who were stolen from us would call to action the rest of America's kids.

Oklahoma's children were the first to respond. I'll never forget when a group of children showed up while we were having lunch, taking a break, early in the operation. We were sitting at a table in the Myriad Convention Center, where we were housing and feeding rescuers, when the children started circulating through the dining room. They had letters and cards they'd made for us, each presented with a hug. By the time the children left, there wasn't a dry eye in the place.

We were totally rejuvenated by the experience, and it was the first of many. Children all over the world began their aggressive campaign to support us. By the weekend, everywhere we went there were stacks of letters and pictures drawn by children. All of them said, "We love you." And "We appreciate you." And "We're with you." We were never alone or felt defeated again. The energy from children all over the world made a difference.

When I say everywhere, I mean everywhere. In chow lines there would be a table with a basket of letters. When we sat down to eat, there was another basket with letters and fruit. Drawings were scattered up and down the tables. Down at the building, in the operations area, there were letters. Banners on the walls. Children hung signs up and down the streets we used getting to and from the building. It was all just very, very touching.

Everyone had their favorite letters, ones that especially touched their hearts. One of mine came from a mother in Rush Springs, Oklahoma, who wrote: "We want you to know how much of an impact your hard work and dedication has had on all Oklahomans. Last night, my two-year-old daughter, Summer, was watching the rescue efforts with me and my husband. Suddenly she turned to me and said, 'I want to be a fireman!' Even a two-year-old understands the value of your efforts—so keep your head up—your spirits up, and hang in there for the victims, the families, the Oklahomans and especially for the children." I can't wait until things slow down enough so I have a little time, because near the top of my list will be saying thanks to the Foster family in Rush Springs. They made a difference for me.

One of the greatest rewards of my life has been the opportunity to visit a number of schools since the end of the search and rescue effort. Most of the ceremonies are similar, but they are each special and unique in their own way. Sometimes kids get up and recite great things they've written ... beautiful words from the heart. Sometimes we have the opportunity to talk with children whose parents died in the explosion. Sometimes there are children of rescue workers in the classes we visit. Who is there and what we do often varies, but two things always stay the same.

Without exception, the kids give the rescue

workers a standing ovation at least once during the ceremony. And without exception, the rescue workers thank them and tell them the truth ... that the kids themselves are among the real heroes. They're the ones who helped us keep our faith in a situation that could have sent us into the depths of despair. I wish everyone in America could experience what we have in those classrooms and gymnasiums. There is genuine mutual respect and affection. On the list of things that make life worth living, I know one that belongs there for sure: there is nothing better than to be loved and admired by children.

6

The Rescuers

THERE HAS BEEN unprecedented attention placed on rescue workers since the bombing of the Alfred P. Murrah Federal Building. The tragedy has caused the entire nation to ask a lot of questions about what they observed over the course of the following weeks.

One of the questions I've been asked repeatedly is just what kind of person wants to be a firefighter. It's usually asked out of respect, but there are also times when I hear a bit of confusion in people's voices. I guess that's understandable.

I'd say that all public safety officers—firefighters, police officers, and state troopers—have to possess a deep yearning to serve their fellow citizens. These guardians must have the unselfish desire to stand ready to put their lives on the line for a total stranger. So I like to tell people that it sincerely takes a special calling to become a public safety professional.

There is a lot of honor in my profession, but there is also a lot of sacrifice. By the very nature of the business, each person is choosing to put himself or herself in harm's way for others.

When the blast happened, all public safety agencies turned out in full force. Other emergency agencies immediately deployed support to the scene. For the first twelve hours, it was Oklahomans who were in the building laboring to find survivors. I'm proud to be part of that group, because they made a difference in people's lives. We were met with the greatest challenge of our careers when we arrived at the Federal Building, but we were prepared and we did a great job.

It was clear within minutes of our arrival that we could use all the assistance we could get. FEMA (Federal Emergency Management Agency) was invited into the city. And the fire chief was then designated to interact directly with FEMA director James Lee Whit.

FEMA immediately activated two Urban Search And Rescue teams (USAR) to travel to Oklahoma City. Both the Phoenix Fire Department and the Sacramento Fire Department were selected because of their special expertise in collapse rescue. Typically, teams are made up primarily of firefighters with expertise in specialized rescues:

collapse, below ground, or high-angle. Joining firefighters, however, are often structural specialists, medical doctors, dog handlers, and other highly trained professionals. We weren't exactly sure what resources these teams would bring to Oklahoma City, but we were glad they were coming.

The Phoenix team arrived the first night and were actually deployed into the building by about two o'clock the next morning. It wasn't until I completed one of our late-night media updates that I discovered the team had arrived. When I walked to the command area, there sat Assistant Fire Chief Dennis Compton of the Phoenix Fire Department. What a welcome sight he was!

Many people don't know it, but most of the time when FEMA/USAR rescue teams travel to another town, the firefighters bear at least part of their own expenses. I'm so proud of our community because that didn't happen here. In fact, one of the stories I'll always remember Governor Keating telling me was about a FEMA rescue worker preparing to return home. Apparently the firefighter walked up to Governor Keating and said, "Governor, before I go home I want to show you an Oklahoma dollar. Do you know what an Oklahoma dollar looks like?"

The Governor said he was puzzled as the firefighter reached into his pocket and pulled out an ordinary-looking dollar bill. "Governor, this is an

Oklahoma dollar. It is the dollar that was in my pocket when I arrived—and because of the generosity of your great citizens—the same dollar is in my pocket as I leave to return home."

Throughout the sixteen days we worked inside the Federal Building, rescue workers came and went from places all across this country. Without exception, each one returned to their home state with a newfound appreciation and special affection for the people of Oklahoma.

People ask me all the time how rescue workers dealt with the physical and mental exhaustion they experienced from being in the building day after day. One way, of course, is the fire department's extensive stress management program. An equally important key to maintaining sanity is our insistence that workers take a break to spend time at home with their families.

In fact, that's one of the primary reasons why FEMA continually rotated teams in and out of the city—because the visiting workers didn't have the balance of being able to go home at night to sleep in their own beds.

I know personally that it makes all the difference in the world.

The first night I got home about three A.M. My wife, Jenifer, had returned home from the television station only minutes before I did. Rather than attempt to sleep for the little time we had before we both headed back to our jobs, we just sat and talked. We reviewed the day's events—

what each of us had done since we'd left home the morning before. This was a chance to unwind for both of us.

Jenifer was interested in what I had to tell her, but I was equally interested in what she had done all day. It was amazing to me to learn that she and her co-anchor had been beamed worldwide in the early hours of the coverage. It took the networks a while to arrive, so until then the local news broadcasts were the world's only link to Oklahoma City.

I had to leave to return to the scene by four-thirty, so we had only about forty-five minutes to talk before I took a shower and changed clothes. Jenifer herself would be able to sleep for only a few hours; she wanted to check on our three-year-old daughter, Jill, who was staying the night with my sister, before she returned to the station. I don't think I had another chance to see Jenifer again until that Saturday night, three days later. We both had a tremendous amount of responsibility during this entire ordeal. Those forty-five minutes Jenifer and I spent together early that morning helped keep me going—kept us both moving—through the days ahead.

Just being at home for that short time reminded me why it was important for the FEMA/ USAR team to be rotated in and out. That doesn't mean it was ever easy to get them to feel good about leaving. Each team felt some ownership in what we were doing, and without fail firefighters wanted to continue working. Not only were they professionals who like to complete a task, they also developed a relationship with Oklahoma City, with this community, and with that building. They hung signs with messages to the people of Oklahoma City in the downtown area, and they left a flag hanging in the building when it was time to go. These men and women became a part of all of us, and prior to leaving town, each team had its own memorial service at the building to say the group's goodbyes. It was clear that when the teams left, they were leaving a part of themselves with us.

It wasn't uncommon to see a firefighter shed a few tears when talking about leaving and going home. All the Oklahoma firefighters understood exactly how they felt. We will never forget those who came to help us search for and recover our loved ones.

Every FEMA/USAR team was unique, and it would be impossible to single out any one team because they were all just unbelievable. However, two stories come to mind to demonstrate the way we all worked together to save one another from despair.

First, I like to tell people about the little shack in front of the building that we constructed out of plywood so that workers could get out of the weather or take a minute to visit. It was a small structure, but it served a multitude of purposes.

Anyway, one morning we arrived at the scene to discover that the men and women from Mont-

gomery County, Maryland, had painted MONTGOM-
ERY COUNTY HILTON on the side of the shack. From
then on you couldn't help but smile every time
you walked by.

Another story that demonstrates the solid nature of the relationships that we built with out-of-
town firefighters came from one of our captains.
He told me that the day the Fairfax, Virginia, team
was leaving for home, he went to the Myriad
Convention Center to thank them for the job
they'd done. Actually, he had planned to talk with
just a few of the firefighters he'd worked with a
lot and ended up visiting with the entire team. As
he turned to walk away and head back to the site,
he stopped short, hearing them clapping behind
him. He turned to see what was happening—only
to discover the team giving him a standing ovation.

One aspect that helped all of us to do our jobs
well was the professionalism and training of everyone involved. Our Oklahoma City district
chiefs were used in the overall building rescue
command. Our special operations coordinator,
District Chief Mike Shannon, had been working
with me to develop a technical rescue system
prior to the blast. Mike was responsible for devel-
oping plans that told us where we would go next
and how we would get there. He would meet
with engineers about structural problems and
coordinate solutions with personnel on each
work shift. The system worked so well, and we
had so much confidence in our team leaders,

Chief Marrs and I got involved only on an as-needed basis.

Add to the competency of our personnel the experience of Mark Ghillarducci from FEMA, Ray Downey from the New York Fire Department, and other USAR team leaders—and you can begin to understand why we were always so confident in our decisions. It was an incredible resource of expertise and input.

Given the chance to write six more books, I could never sufficiently commend the men and women who make up the Oklahoma City Fire Department. They went above and beyond the call of duty time after time. Over the twenty-two years I have served in the city's fire department, I have had the chance to spend time with many of these colleagues and I'm always impressed with their spirit.

This professional challenge offered yet another opportunity to show what these people are made of. They toiled for days surrounded by death, yet never lost heart or sight of the goal. They pulled together to staff our stations throughout the city because we had to continue to maintain fire service for the rest of the community. It's nothing short of impressive how these people united to meet the incredible responsibilities thrust on them in the blink of an eye.

It would be too cumbersome to detail what each of these public servants did for their city during this national disaster, but every one of the approximately one thousand individuals who work for the department played a significant role. Early on, every related city, county, and state agency joined forces to try to rescue survivors, but the recovery was done primarily by firefighters from the metro area, along with the FEMA/USAR teams. These two groups were active in the bulk of the operation, and they almost exclusively bore the responsibility of removing bodies from the debris.

Does any one person stand out as deserving special recognition for contribution to the rescue effort? If I were to start such a list, it would have to begin with Chief Marrs. The fire chief took control of the incident from the word go. He demonstrated his leadership and made organization a priority. He took command not merely by instructing people with *you do this* or *you do that*. His leadership was focused on the bigger issues in front of us: mobilizing personnel, getting resources, and establishing the command system. I was proud to work alongside him to set up an organizational structure that would prove to serve us well throughout the entire operation.

Any others? As I said before, if I started with one, I'd have to list all one thousand plus men and women who make up the Oklahoma City Fire Department. How do you recognize firefighters who worked moving a hundred tons of rubble each day without recognizing their colleagues who made it possible for them to be there—the men and women protecting the rest of the city, preventing and investigating fires, dispatching crews, and maintaining our equipment. Each performed an equally valuable role and each is deserving of the public's trust and appreciation.

It's important to state that by the second and third day we had numerous rescue personnel arriving on their own initiative. In each case, we did our best to incorporate as many of them as we could into the effort. There were limits on how many people could be inside at any given time due to the extensive structural damage, so, on occasion, we had to turn away some units. Firefighters arriving in groups of two or ten were a testimony to the deep commitment and unlimited courage of the men and women who protect their communities every day.

Law enforcement officers were our partners and our friends throughout the entire rescue operation. They protected the premises, keeping us safe. They were involved in major decisions and provided their support to any decision that was made. Many found their way inside during the first hours after the bombing, and it was not uncommon to find an officer and a firefighter working hand in hand.

There were two Oklahoma City police officers who often dressed in protective clothing, joining firefighters throughout the operation. Sergeant Lynn McCumber and Officer Frank Koch earned eternal respect from the entire search and rescue team for their dedication and staying power.

On Friday, just two days after the bombing,

word spread through the building that a prime suspect in the bombing was apprehended by Oklahoma State Trooper Charlie Hanger. That sent a wave of energy through the crew on duty. It was an instant uplift. There were high-fives, shouts of relief, and cries for swift justice—everything you'd expect from men and women coping with the source of the pain and anguish that was now gripping our community. A sigh of relief—and then right back to work. Celebrations were something meant for another day. Our work was still our number-one priority.

Rescue workers were tenacious about sorting through the chaos. It was hard to get anyone to leave the building—even at shift change. Crew members would repeatedly say, "Let me just finish moving this bit of debris before I go." Or: "Let's just get through this one last piece of rebar." Any excuse they could find. That's the type of dedication those rescue workers demonstrated.

It was for their own safety, and on the advice of on-site medical staff that we continually rotated workers out of the building. Not only for the obvious physical reasons, but mental reasons as well. I've said it a hundred times since the incident, the rescuers continually served in harm's way, striving to get the job done without regard to personal safety.

There was a tremendous amount of dust and airborne particles that caused dry nasal passages, sore throats, or headaches. We were repeatedly changing the type of dust masks and filtering systems being used.

Early on, two rescue workers encountered minor injuries. Neither was seriously hurt, but both were sent home for a few days. After that we noticed that reports of injuries decreased. Workers with small abrasions and cuts would hide them. They would get something in their eye, wash it out, and return to work. They worked with headaches. They worked nauseated. They would work with a sore ankle or sore knee or sore back. All because they wanted to be there. Rescuers knew if they reported any injury or complaint to an EMS person or one of the physicians on site, they would risk having to leave the building. That possibility was considered worse than any discomfort they were experiencing.

How does one retain one's humanity after what we saw inside that building? It's a sensitive issue and that's why rescuers went through our stress management program as they came out of the building after each shift. What happens when we meet is totally confidential. As firefighters, we completely respect the privacy of these sessions. We worked diligently to develop the relationships and trust that made those counseling sessions successful. So, accordingly, it wasn't appropriate to talk about what happened when we meet— what I or anyone else said or felt. The only constant about the program was that everyone participated—even Chief Marrs and myself.

Most days I got my meals at One Bell Central because it was convenient and because our fire chaplain was stationed there. I also usually invited Major Rick Williams, Major John Long, Major Sheila Hays, and anyone working in the area to participate in a critical incident stress management discussion. We simply sat and talked while we ate our meal together. What we talked about was a very private matter. That's why this type of stress management works.

Being a rescue worker at the Federal Building meant forcing yourself to detach from the familiar for sixteen days straight. It would have been impossible to restrict the search to workers who had no connection to the building. Like the rest of the community, most of us had some sort of direct association with one or more of the employees who worked there. I remember going to the Social Security office a few years back to get a card for Jill. I remember when the day care center opened and it was reported in the press. Fire service personnel had been in and out of that building doing a pre-fire plan. We knew faces of people we'd seen while doing our job. Relatives of fellow firefighters worked there. Friends of friends were missing after the blast. The connections were very real and constantly present.

Some asked during the rescue effort if our personal connections to people in the building made our crews the best or worst to be doing the job. There are opinions both ways, and I suspect that even mental health professionals would differ. I personally believe there was a lot of extra motivation driving our troops. Not only did they have a job to do, they had a job to do for people they knew, respected, and, in some instances, loved.

We were aware of media reports in which attorneys assigned to defend a bombing suspect asked to be removed from the case because they had personal friends in the building and felt that they could not be objective. We didn't judge them, because being objective is a critical part of doing their jobs. Frankly, it isn't a requirement for us. Our job demands professionalism and discipline, but caring about our victims is part of what moves us forward.

Where we drew the line was with family members. There were two firefighters who had a daughter and a sister in the building, and neither was allowed to work at the site. That would have been much too personal. That would have been much too difficult—for them and for us.

Oklahoma City Lieutenant Kenneth Adams lost his daughter and future grandchild in the blast. After the funeral, some members of our department did escort him down to look at the scene. He wanted to see it, and we felt it was appropriate. Kenny has over twenty years of service in the Oklahoma City Fire Department, and he was clearly a part of the rescue team in spirit. So we proudly escorted Kenny to the site.

* * *

It took a tremendous amount of discipline to move deep into the building the morning of the blast. Fortunately, the urgency of the situation created a special energy. Professional sports figures are familiar with such situations. We've all heard the Oklahoma Sooners talk about the sensation of walking down the ramp at the Cotton Bowl when they play the University of Texas Longhorns. We've heard athletes tell us about the adrenaline rush they feel at events like the Super Bowl, the World Series, or the NBA Finals. They're pumped and they're ready to play ball.

Well, the adrenaline rush we experienced was something like that because we knew we were facing the toughest moment in our careers. We were psyched up and ready to help the people inside the building. But the feeling was also as different as night and day.

This adrenaline rush came with a strong dose of reality. This was no sporting event. There was nothing fun about what we were facing. We were dealing with life-and-death situations. We knew that our actions and our performance within the next five minutes, the next thirty minutes, the next hour, would have mortal consequences. This was no game. We knew that.

Seasoned veterans made an added contribution that day. They modeled discipline and skills for others to follow. These experienced firefighters had been in tough situations before, when life was hanging in the balance, and they understood how to handle the pressure.

It's difficult to describe, but I continue to try because I want people to understand what it was like in there—and the magnitude of what firefighters were facing every single day. There's an old adage among veteran firefighters—that the story can be told only by the men and women inside. No one has ever come up with adequate words to clearly tell what it's like to be in the bowels of a major inferno. And that's exactly the same situation I find myself in as I attempt to describe what it was like inside the Murrah Building. You don't want to exclude people or set yourself apart by insisting that you had to be there to experience it. But maybe that's true.

In watching the news accounts, you might have asked yourself why firefighters weren't running back and forth from the site—why they always seemed to be walking, quickly and deliberately, yes, but still walking. Well, it's part of our training and the discipline I frequently mention. We understand the importance of being sure-footed. We understand that remaining calm when confronted by chaos is critical to our effectiveness. Escalating our heart rates will only drain us of the energy we'll require seconds later. We cannot allow our hearts and minds to yield to the panic around us.

Yes, we walk. We don't run. But we get there immediately, prepared to perform. To systematically address the problem in front of us. It's proven to be a successful strategy for fire service personnel all across this country, and it served us well when we encountered the carnage at the Murrah Federal Building at Fifth and Harvey.

Another phenomenon that happens to rescuers on the job is that they lose all sense of time. In this situation, there was the hustle and bustle of fellow rescuers, medical personnel, law enforcement officers, and volunteers. We were strategically placing equipment and setting up systems. Ambulances and people were racing to and from the scene. Everything around us was fast-forwarding into a blur of activity.

But at the time for those of us working inside the building, the experience was something like watching a videotape playing in slow motion. We encountered tons and tons of debris, all of which had to be removed one piece at a time. It was hard enough to locate a survivor, or even a victim, in the midst of such heavy destruction. And finding victims was only the beginning of the problem. Once we found a person, dead or alive, we had to uncover them. I know of situations where it took four and five hours to free someone from the debris that trapped them. Things were very fast-paced, but the task was so tedious, it was sometimes difficult to see progress.

In long-term perspective, the condition of the site wasn't the most unbelievable part of this experience. That distinction goes to the family members. We were constantly in awe of these individuals who were so caring toward us in the face of all they lost. Every time we visited the family center, people asked about the safety of those working in the building. Anytime family members encountered rescue workers directly, they were quick to ask how the rescuers were doing.

I guess you could say they treated us as partners struggling through this horrific experience together. It meant the world to us that they would allow us to share in their grief.

When you are working to rescue someone, in some ways you become a part of that person. Your actions on their behalf form a special bond.

Well, in this case, we did join with the victims in the Murrah Building, but that was a very painful experience because most of the people we were able to recover had died in the blast. It eased our pain to be cared for by these victims' families. They in turn became an extension of our own families.

Since the end of the rescue effort, many of the rescue workers have struggled with the hero status that the public continues to foist on us. While we were working we were somewhat isolated from what the community was thinking. Frankly, it came as a surprise to many that over the course of the sixteen days, the public had watched us with such deep respect. We felt we went into the building regular Oklahomans and came out changed—but still everyday, ordinary citizens. The heroes' welcome we've received was somewhat unexpected; in our judgment we were merely doing our job. We are deeply honored by the response of our community and the nation. And we are proud to stand with the real heroes: the men and women who volunteered their time, as an example of what is good and right about this country.

7

Satellite City

As you could tell from the dramatic pictures that were seen on television and in newspapers across the country, the local media arrived on the scene within minutes of the blast. Of course, that's understandable. In the case of our local television affiliates, all the stations were close enough—just six miles away—to feel the blast and see the windows shake on their buildings. Information was immediately available in the newsrooms, as they all have scanners to monitor our radio traffic.

Local police and highway patrol officials gave the initial media news briefings as both Chief Marrs and I were working feverishly to set up the command center and initiate rescue operations. Since the fire department was in charge of all rescue and recovery efforts, it wasn't long until the media began requesting time to talk with someone from our department.

Accordingly, I went to the building to get an updated and accurate status report and to check on the progress of our special operations team, which I am also responsible for. Once I returned to the media area and did my first interview, it became clear to me that our department would be the one with the information the media would be most interested in over the coming days.

We had established an area where the transfer of information could take place, but the location had to be changed a number of times that first day for safety reasons. I'm certain that was as frustrating for our friends in the news media as it was for us. Overall, the working media was very cooperative, even though moving locations was no easy task for them. It meant disconnecting and repositioning satellite links and live trucks, neither of which is an easy feat.

It was critical that all journalists be given equal access to information at precisely the same time. So the creation of a media center was something we had paid attention to early on, settling in an area two blocks northwest of the Federal Building. The front border line was an alley between Sixth Street and Seventh Street, just west of Harvey. As the area was slightly elevated, it provided a reasonably good view. Most cameras could capture images of the building from the fourth floor up, with the lower floors and the pancake area pretty much blocked from view by other buildings in the foreground.

We were sensitive to the media's need for a "good shot," as it is called, so the public could relate to what was happening. We also had to be considerate of the rescue workers, victims, and the victims' families. In the end, everyone was convinced that we had their best interests at heart, so the location we selected satisfied all.

The first time I realized that anyone outside Oklahoma City was watching the rescue effort was when a local TV reporter told me that their coverage was being fed to the national network as well as to CNN. This situation was news being telecast worldwide.

One of our local TV stations was the first entity to video the disaster from the air, providing extraordinary footage for the world to see. Based on what he saw on television from the helicopter shots, Governor Keating immediately issued a "declaration of disaster."

Within one hour of the incident, all our local stations had live trucks or satellite uplinks in place. At the time, they didn't remotely suspect that they were setting up for coverage that would extend over the next sixteen days. Because it took the out-of-state journalists a few hours to begin arriving, the local media secured and maintained prime placement throughout the incident.

My first interviews consisted of the most basic information: that rescuers were in the building, who those rescuers were, that EMSA crews were on site performing triage, giving treatment, and providing transportation. We also reported that area hospitals had implemented their respective disaster plans and that we were doing our utmost to shepherd the walking wounded and to remove survivors trapped in the building.

One of our immediate concerns was that people would attempt to come to the building to see what had happened, thereby clogging up the roadways for emergency vehicles. The news media was extremely helpful about asking people to avoid the downtown area so that the rescue effort could move as quickly as possible. When cellular phone circuits were jammed, broadcasters urged the public to stay off mobile phones so that emergency and rescue workers could communicate with one another. To provide information to the families of potential victims, we asked the Red Cross to set up an information hotline and the media repeatedly broadcast the number.

It was incredible to observe. The media was amazingly quick to relay our every request. In those early hours media management took the position that their job was not only to report the story, but to assist in the rescue effort as well. Reporters worked together, sharing information, and soliciting resources as they were needed.

There are dozens of examples of media support. One related to safety was demonstrated when we were having trouble evacuating the Regency Tower, a high-rise apartment complex that had sustained extensive damage as a result of the blast. We asked the media to broadcast the message that residents of the Regency Tower should evacuate the building in an orderly manner. That request helped our firefighters who were going floor by floor searching for injured people and for structural damage.

Anytime we asked, reporters were also eager to help broadcast updates for needed supplies. Before we had time to set up systems to obtain supplies from local relief agencies, this support was invaluable. Ironically, the only drawback was the public's overwhelming generosity. Whenever we requested something, we always got far more than we needed of each and every item.

Our covenant with the media was that we would always provide them with factual and up-to-date information. Initially, the only people who did interviews from the fire department were Chief Marrs and I. We ensured that we were providing accurate and consistent information. He and I met regularly to compare notes and to update each other with the most current facts and figures. The chief represented our department at the formal national news conferences each day, speaking in conjunction with the leaders of all the other agencies involved on the scene. Providing periodic updates from the site and meeting any specific requests from the media became my responsibility. Special media requests were organized by Major Rick Williams, who became our media assistant at the site. I did everything humanly possible to honor every commitment we made.

By the second day, we had nicknamed the media area "satellite city," as there was almost a two-square-block area of nothing but satellite trucks and live trucks lined up side by side. Several prestigious network television journalists told me that in their long careers they had never seen that many media trucks covering any single incident, including the O. J. Simpson trial. A number of reporters commented that there hadn't been this much media attention focused on one event since the assassination of President Kennedy back in 1963.

Soon, regular coverage was not providing enough information to satisfy the public's appetite for news from the scene. Invitations began pouring in from *Nightline*, NBC's *Dateline*, and other special news magazine shows. CNN was asking for more frequent updates as they, along with our local affiliates, were providing round-the-clock coverage. There was no precedent for the extensive coverage we received from our local television stations. It was the following week before they returned to any significant amount of regular programming.

As more and more reporters arrived from all across the country, I admit that I was in awe. On the other side of the microphones and tape recorders were the voices and faces we all know from *Nightline*, *20/20*, *Dateline*, *48 Hours*, and other shows. It was incredible to imagine that all

OKLAHOMA RESCUE

An early glimpse of the bomb's mass destruction.

©*The Daily Oklahoman*, photo by Jim Argo

Lieutenant Cecil Clay responds to the Federal Building crisis.

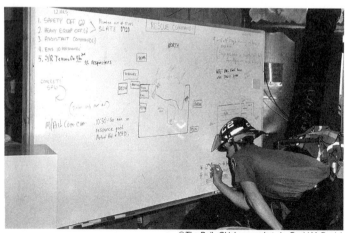

©*The Daily Oklahoman*, photo by David McDaniel

The Oklahoma City Fire Operations Board inside the Federal Building.

Assistant Fire Chief Jon Hansen stands under reinforcements in cave area.

Operations shack in front of the Federal Building.

Special Operations Coordinator Mike Shannon enters the cave.

Nine floors of debris pancaked in front of the Federal Building.

Firefighters make entry into a void space in the pancake.

©*The Daily Oklahoman,* photo by David McDaniel

©*The Daily Oklahoman,* photo by David McDaniel

A rescue worker assists an injured child.

Oklahoma City Fire Chief Gary Marrs briefs national media.

©*The Daily Oklahoman*, photo by Steve Cooch   ©*The Daily Oklahoman*, photo by Jim Argo

©*The Daily Oklahoman*, photo by David McDaniel

A construction worker helps to secure the damaged structure.

Heavy steel bracing being carried into the pit area.

Welding steel braces to provide safety for workers.

Working to shore up the pit area.

©*The Daily Oklahoman*, photo by David McDaniel

Major Craig Rolke with wreath placed by rescuers at the front of the Federal Building.

Assistant Fire Chief Jon Hansen reflecting on his conversations with family members at the site.

these national reporters were gathered in Oklahoma City.

All of the national publications and large metropolitan newspapers were here in full force as well. The major news magazines had large crews covering the story. It was certainly a different experience to have print journalists approach me for an interview, saying they were from *The New York Times* or *The Dallas Morning News* or *The Washington Post.* Just as unusual was talking to reporters from *Newsweek, Time, U.S. News and World Report*, and *People.*

Many of the cities that had sent FEMA/USAR teams also sent reporters. We paid particular attention to their needs because we wanted citizens from those communities to know how deeply grateful we were that they sent their firefighters to assist us. We invited members of the individual search and rescue teams to the media area to talk with their local reporters so some of the messages sent back to cities came directly from their own rescue personnel.

Media restrictions existed in the covering of this situation that have not been imposed in other large-scale disasters such as areas hit by hurricanes, earthquakes, floods, or tornadoes. The reason, of course, was because this was also a crime scene of gigantic proportions with massive amounts of evidence and leads that had to be protected by federal investigators. Within the first hour after the bombing, a secured perimeter had been set up around the mass murder scene.

Although members of the media respected it, the limitation was also frustrating to them.

It was difficult for reporters to capture the sights and sounds of the incident—to feel what rescue workers were going through, to get a close-up view of the destruction caused by the bomb. For people charged with creating pictures and verbal images for the public, I know it was sometimes hard for them to rely on us for descriptions, especially since we often had a difficult time putting into words what we were experiencing. It's a cliché for sure, but a picture really is worth a thousand words.

People ask me all the time, now that the rescue effort is over, which reporter I liked the most. That would be hard to say. Of course, I have a great fondness for our local media, as they are friends as well as professional associates. As for the others, what a humbling experience to be interviewed by dozens of reporters I'd only seen or read about. It was a unique cast of characters that gathered in Oklahoma City for sixteen days, and it was interesting to meet and talk with each and every one of them.

Without slighting any of the reporters, I will say that Harry Smith from CBS is one of the kindest people I've ever met. He was always personal and genuine. I could tell that he really cared—and cared deeply—about what was happening in and to Oklahoma City.

Roger O'Neil of NBC is the person from the national media that I'd have to say I connected with the most. I liked him personally, but it was more than that. When we decided to take a national pool of reporters into the building, Roger was selected. We dressed him in full protective clothing and walked him through what rescue workers were doing to search for and recover victims. Sharing that experience with him formed a special connection between us, because I knew he understood what I was saying in a way that only someone who had been inside might comprehend.

Ted Koppel of ABC really felt for the people in Oklahoma City. Though I didn't meet him personally, I could hear the compassion in his voice when we talked over the airways.

Bernard Shaw from CNN was an amazing person to me. Because he spent so much time covering the Gulf War, he knew what bombed-out buildings looked like and the devastation bombs can cause. When asked what he believed was a comparable story, he said he had never covered anything like this with the possible exception of the Jim Jones massacre in Guyana.

Bryant Gumbel of NBC is a guy who does his homework. When he arrived on the scene he walked up to me and said, "Hi, Jon. How's your wife, Jenifer?" Having never met the man, I couldn't help but be impressed.

Tom Brokaw from NBC is also someone who touched me personally. He asked good, informed questions about the fire service, and was very complimentary of our firefighters. Clearly, he knew something about our profession, so it was all the more meaningful when he told me that he believes it takes a special person to be a firefighter.

Two other out-of-state reporters come to mind. The first was Amy Jacobson from WJBK-TV in Detroit, Michigan. Amy wrote me that a week after she returned home she was still feeling a great sense of loss and sadness. Her comments served to reconfirm for me the personal connection she and the people of her state had with this story.

Another crew that I will always remember is the one that came all the way from Seattle, Washington. I had met them earlier this year when I traveled to their state to participate in a memorial for several of their fallen firefighters who had died in the line of duty. Now here they were coming all the way to Oklahoma to interview our firefighters about what was happening in our lives. It just reminded me how close the entire fire service community is, and the realization made it an extra pleasure to do interviews with the Seattle crew.

I'd almost gotten used to the fact that I'd be talking daily with national figures like Tom Brokaw, Harry Smith, and Ted Koppel, when I was stopped in my tracks again. A gentleman I didn't recognize approached me, saying, "Pardon me, sir. Would you have a moment to talk to the BBC?" I'd have to say that was yet another time when I realized how many millions of people were watching what was happening in Oklahoma. After that I found it hard to be surprised by anything.

Media arrived from all over the world, and I talked with most of them personally. Specifically, I remember doing interviews with TV crews from Spain, Great Britain, Australia, France, Norway, Korea—countries on every continent around the world. Radio stations from even more countries came to provide their citizens with firsthand accounts.

By day three there were so many media crews here, people began calling the camera staging area "media row." It was difficult to stand in one place where everyone could have access, so when we did an update, I would move down the rows of reporters so everyone could receive the same information.

I'll never forget something that happened as I was working my way down the line one afternoon. I had already finished three or four briefs, when a petite young lady who had been very patient finally made her way to the front to say, "But, excuse me, sir. Do you have time for French TV?" It was so understated, I had to smile. She had traveled so far and all she wanted was a few minutes of time. "Well, yes, ma'am," I said, and we had the interview.

There were two crews that I was particularly proud to talk to: Norwegian television and radio teams. They noticed that my last name was Hansen with an *e*, and asked me if I was of Norwegian heritage. When I told them I was, it was like

111

a special bridge between me and their viewers. I was very moved by the chance to talk directly with the people who share my family's history.

One of the most interesting reporters was Boris Notkin, the Russian journalist. The questions he asked were different from everyone else's. He asked about the political system and why the two political parties weren't blaming each other for what happened. I asked him if he found the building as staggering as we all did. I'll never forget what he said. "If you see the capital of Grozny with six hundred thousand people, and half of it looks exactly like this, you wouldn't be much impressed by one single building. But the response of the people really makes me admire the Americans."

Daily he lives with the reality of bombs in his homeland. What he found so remarkable in Oklahoma was our people's regard for human life.

The days grew longer as the rescue effort continued. It wasn't uncommon to start a day with one of the network morning shows and to end it with a late-night program like *Nightline*. It made for some exhausting days because there were also endless responsibilities in between.

Our entire media operation had to rely on mutual respect for it to be successful. We dealt with the media with integrity and honor, and that respect was returned to us by reporters. Over the years our fire department had worked hard to develop a positive rapport and even a kind of trust with our local media. We were committed to building the same solid relationships with the national media. Being accurate, telling the truth, and honoring our commitments to fulfill their requests—those were the three objectives in our media strategy. There were times when something happened in the building that caused us to miss interviews, but even then the media was amicable. None of us ever lost sight of what the priority was: search, rescue, and recovery operations.

When did we brief the media? Frankly, we let them set the schedule for formal briefings, as they were the ones with the deadlines. Time zones made the dissemination of information even more complicated. What was a good time to ensure that a deadline could be met for one person was often a terrible time for someone else. Finally, we set up structured briefing times:

4:30 A.M.	National news
5:00 A.M.	Local affiliates
10:00 A.M.	Formal briefing by the fire chief, FBI, police chief, public works director, FEMA director, etc.
11:00 A.M.	Status of the rescue operation
3:00 P.M.	Status of the rescue operation
4:00 P.M.	Status of the rescue operation

Those were the times for standard reports, but we talked with the media a great deal more than that. Anytime we had a change in the operations, or we had a structural problem, or the fatality count went up, we would do our best to bring the news media up to speed in a timely fashion.

We also made the decision to take pool cameras inside the building. That's when only one camera would go inside but the resulting photos or video had to be shared with everybody else on the scene. That meant that whoever went in with us was required to book satellite time, "putting the information up on the bird," as the media people described it. The pool concept, of course, required us to secure permission from the FBI and all the other law enforcement agencies since the building was classified as a mass murder crime scene.

We did what it took to get the media inside, however, because we believed that the rescue workers needed the public to understand why the operation was moving so slowly. We wanted America to see how tough each step of the way was for rescuers. We wanted people to see workers removing debris by hand and to observe the tremendous amount of shoring that was required to keep rescuers out of harm's way. Those who went inside were deeply moved and somewhat afraid for their own safety—and rightly so.

I guess it would be impossible to get that many reporters together for anything without running the risk of rumors and inaccurate stories. There were rumors that Geraldo Rivera had dressed up in a uniform so that he could get into the area. I'm not certain what clothes he wore when, but

I can tell you that he never made it into the restricted area.

There were rumors that unnamed federal law enforcement officials stopped the search and rescue effort in order to retrieve key documents. With many victims in federal law enforcement–related agencies, workers had friends and loved ones in the building, so that idea is ludicrous. At no time did they hamper any rescue efforts, and to the contrary, they did their best to help.

It is true that the rescue effort came to a halt when a TV tabloid reporter made his way into the restricted area. That person was quickly caught and arrested.

I guess the media story everyone wants to hear about is the interview with Connie Chung for the *CBS Evening News.* Connie had just arrived in town and was driven in her limousine to the site for the national news update. Just a short time later, she was interviewing me live when she turned and asked point-blank, "Can you [the Oklahoma City Fire Department] handle this?"

My initial reaction was certainly surprise, because that's exactly what we'd been doing, and doing well, since 9:02 A.M. I had done dozens of interviews by that time and no other member of the press had questioned our ability to deal with the crisis. At the time, I didn't really take offense. I simply answered what seemed to be a silly question as politely as possible.

I had no idea at the time that her doubts about our department would so deeply offend many of my fellow Oklahomans and even the rest of the nation. By the time she was interviewing me, cities and states all over the country were feeling great empathy with Oklahoma City, and the public rushed to our defense. They had watched our hard work for hours and knew that our rescue workers were doing an incredible job.

Did I think at the time the question was a little inappropriate? Yes, I did. Emotions were running high, and the question was certainly insensitive to the moment. Citizens here have always felt a pride of ownership in the fire department, and after watching the rescuers at work all day on April 19, they interpreted her remark as degrading and frankly ridiculous. It hurt our citizens in ways that even I didn't realize at the time.

It wasn't until the next day that I realized the problem that Ms. Chung had created for herself. People began saying they were offended by the way she had treated me in the interview. To tell you the truth, I had to think back about what she said. I was doing so many interviews that they were all running together in my mind. The anti–Connie Chung T-shirts that showed up on the streets downtown sent a message to CBS that the problem wasn't going to go away easily.

The news director from our local CBS affiliate contacted me two days after my first on-air conversation with Ms. Chung, saying that Connie wanted the opportunity to try and set things right in a live TV interview with me. I agreed to do the interview later that day, though it was very awkward for several reasons. Obviously, the last thing I needed at the time was to be in conflict with a major network news anchor. On top of that, my wife works for the CBS affiliate that was requesting the satellite rematch. Fortunately the interview would be refereed by another anchor.

Before I talked with Ms. Chung again, I talked with our fire rescue personnel and asked their opinion about how they wanted me to respond to her remark. Almost to the individual they were saying, "Chief, you know we have to stay focused on what we're doing. Let bygones be bygones. Just let it go." So that's what I did.

Ms. Chung was very apologetic when the cameras rolled this time, and she told the people of Oklahoma that she hadn't meant to slight them in any way. I suspect she was sincere at the time, but it must not have been enough.

Several weeks later, on Saturday, May 20, CBS would oust Ms. Chung from the anchor desk, leaving Dan Rather to preside solo over the *CBS Evening News*. Local citizens were quick to assume that the Oklahoma City interview had played a part in her demise, but no doubt there were other factors as well. I was amazed then—and still am—that it turned into such a big deal.

I realize that coming from New York, Ms. Chung probably looked at the situation and wondered if the job was too big for the Oklahoma City Fire Department. The thought never even occurred to me. Apparently she felt it was her responsibility to ask me what she believed were tough questions. I saw the public get tough as they responded to her question with a huge outpouring of support and respect for the fire-fighters searching for survivors.

Was her question insensitive? That is a question the American public answered for us all, and I was deeply touched by their answer.

8

Common Bond, Uncommon Strength

OVER THE COURSE of sixteen days, the entire nation was completely focused on what was happening at the Federal Building. It wasn't until the search and rescue effort was completed that I began to realize just how differently those of us at the site had seen the situation.

Clearly, our responsibilities inside the building provided us with a unique perspective of what had happened throughout the rescue operation. Like everyone else, we had watched the number of deaths mount as the days passed. We formed a very personal bond with the victims of this tragedy as we worked to return their bodies to their families.

In my conversations since the end of the rescue effort I've been amazed by how much the people of Oklahoma City also connected with the victims. They know many of the names of those who lost their lives in the building. They know their personal stories, where they worked, what they did on their time off.

For example, those who followed the tragedy in the media came to know Susan Ferrell as the beautiful woman who was an attorney for the U.S. Department of Housing and Urban Development. She loved cats, people, traveling, and dancing.

But for those of us who worked inside, listening to the telling of these stories now is like hearing people converse in a foreign language. Though we were intimately involved in the rescue and recovery of each person, we didn't know their names. In fact, part of what we did was to collect personal effects from the area where we found bodies in order to help others learn their names in the identification process.

Even in those instances where we brought people out alive, rarely did rescuers know their full names. Rather, we were focused on removing each person from the debris, administering emergency care, and getting that survivor out of the building to waiting medical professionals. With the number of people we rescued and with what little we knew about each person, it is difficult now to go back and match the people we encountered with the people we heard about in news accounts. From the time we turned people over to medical teams or the medical examiner, we lost track of them.

Sometimes when we were working to free

someone we would ask their first name so we could reassure them. You know, "Brandy, we are here ... we are going to help you. Brandy, hang on. We're going to get you out of this. You're going to be okay. We're from the fire department and we're not going to leave you."

In the days immediately after the initial tragedy, firefighters began telephoning the administration office asking how they could find the name of a person they rescued. Or the name that went with a body they retrieved near the south stairwell.

Survivors who were assisted from the building by a firefighter or police officer or state trooper or sheriff's deputy also phoned. "How do I get in touch to express my gratitude?" That is the common question.

Families called the office as well—with requests to meet the men and women who helped provide their loved ones with a proper goodbye. "Do you know who the rescuers were in our case?" "Do you know who brought our loved one out of the building?"

We have tried to make those connections for people. And we've had some very happy reunions. In fact, I had the opportunity to be at Fire Station No. 5 when Brian Espe came by to meet his rescuer. One of our lieutenants, Mark Ollman, had talked him down our 135-foot ladder at the scene. We set the ladder back up at the station and invited him to climb it again for old time's sake. He didn't even think twice before answering, "No, thanks. I've had my successful trip down the ladder."

It was a great experience for everyone who was there—putting a name with a face that you will never forget for as long as you live. By just this one experience, we became convinced that it was worth the effort to keep trying to reunite as many people as possible.

In two cases, however, no reunion was necessary because the families involved were connected to our entire department. Early on, this tragedy became very personal for every firefighter as two of our colleagues had family members missing.

It was midafternoon the first day when I learned that the twenty-six-year-old daughter of one of our firefighters, Kenneth Adams, was in the building at the time of the blast. Several months pregnant, she worked in the east end of the building on the ninth floor, an area that took a severe amount of the damage.

Her father is not only a colleague, but he is also a good personal friend. He and I served together in the same fire district. We've fought fires side by side. The report I was given said that she was "missing." I hoped with everything in me that she would be found and found alive. I knew if he lost her as a result of this madness, his loss would be our loss. I knew that if she wasn't found alive, my friend would lose both his daughter and his grandchild-to-be. It was unbearable to think that Kenny could lose so much in one single moment.

I'll never forget standing with Kenny at the memorial service for all of the families in front of the building. I put my arm around him and he put his arm around me. He told me, "You know, usually she was late to work—and she didn't have to be there until nine A.M. But she went in early that morning because she was so proud of her new ultrasound pictures. She wanted to show them to her friends before she settled in to do her tasks for the day. That's why she was there at 9:02 A.M. I've asked myself time and again, why couldn't she have been late to work that day?" I understand why he was asking the question, but it was a question that had no answer.

Also, on the first day of the rescue, I learned that we had another firefighter who had a sister in the building. Curtis Froh is a model young firefighter, both mentally and physically. He's a guy who has always been widely admired by his coworkers—and by his sisters. It just didn't seem fair that this person who works daily to save lives should have to suffer the loss of someone he loves.

When the medical examiner notified Curtis's family that his sister's body had been identified as one of the victims of the bombing, it was again a moment of personal grief for all of us in the fire department.

It's important for me to report that every single

rescue worker treated victims with complete honor and respect. Not one rescuer ever lost sight of the fact that each body they recovered was somebody's father, mother, daughter, son, sister, brother, grandparent, or lifelong friend.

Throughout the entire operation, there was a lot of reverence inside the building. There was tremendous regard for the people who had so senselessly lost their lives. Tributes were constantly being paid. It was not uncommon for rescuers to stop and pay their respects when they found a victim. Regardless of the safety risk, they would remove their helmets, bow their heads for a moment, wipe a tear, put their helmets back on, and return to the job at hand.

At times it seemed that the public grew impatient waiting for us to deliver bodies to the medical examiner so that families could be notified. We understood the impatience, but it was equally, if not more, frustrating for the crews inside. Mounds of steel and concrete were stacked so high we felt lucky to find even an arm or leg showing to let us know where to begin. Even when we did locate a body, it often took four or five hours to disentangle it.

From the beginning, I was constantly asked to describe the condition of the bodies we were finding. I guess there was something in most people that wanted to know. Part of it was a lack of understanding about what a bomb would do to people who were unfortunate enough to be caught in its blast.

There were those in other agencies who made graphic comments about the condition bodies were in. I never would discuss it. It was a conscious decision on my part. The reason? A deep respect for the victims who died and equal respect for their families—and the grief they were already doomed to live with for the rest of their lives. People saw pictures of the building, both inside and out, and those of us at the fire department who were making decisions determined early on that we would let the violence of the blast speak for itself.

I'll never forget the first time I went to visit with the victims' families at the First Christian Church. Others had been delivering information about victims and survivors for several days when Lieutenant Gerald Davison of the Oklahoma Highway Patrol asked me to go with him to visit with the families personally. I forget what day it was, but I remember it was an afternoon, about four o'clock. I was apprehensive. The public servant in me wanted desperately to be helpful, but I dreaded looking directly into the faces of those families who had lost so much and had the potential to lose so much more. All the way over there, I was distracted, thinking through what I might say, and fortunately, by the time I arrived, I believed I had it figured out.

We were barely in the front door when I looked up and saw a good friend across the room. I'd known him since high school, and the fact that he was there stopped me suddenly in my tracks. What now? In an instant this nightmare was once again very personal.

Some of the families had brought to the church pictures of their loved ones and they were displayed together as a reminder of why we were all there. For a person who tries always to be prepared, I wondered to myself if I was prepared for this.

I felt honored to be in the presence of those family members. It was important to me to give them reliable information, at least what I could. There was a lot we had to say and many questions to answer. Giving the status report was easy, as I'd provided some of the same information to the media only an hour before. Explaining why things were moving so slowly was much tougher here because I knew how much patience the situation had already demanded from these good people.

I wanted to give them a perspective different from any they'd heard before. Having spent countless hours inside the building with the rescue workers, I could honestly tell them that the thoughts and prayers of those working hour by hour were with them.

Having finished my comments, I had the chance while others spoke to reflect about where I was and what I was doing. This visit completed the circle for me personally. I had seen it all at the site, and now I had been in the presence of the families. It was a very solemn moment.

Then something happened that caught me

completely off guard. As we prepared to leave, the entire room of people began to applaud. Tears rushed to my eyes. I stood there in amazement as the men, women, and children worked their way toward us, asking us to tell the rescue workers that they loved them. Several said please tell them to be careful because they didn't want any of them to get hurt. They handed each of us ribbons with little angel pins on them, ribbons they had personally made for each of the rescuers. We knew that they wanted to be in that building with us, and the pins would serve as a reminder that their hearts were with us wherever we went, whatever we found. In fact, someone handed me a large box to take back to the others who were working. I was proud to carry the handmade treasures back and the rescuers were proud to wear them. Bonds formed between the victims' families and rescue workers, bonds that will never be broken.

Chief Marrs went with me on my next visit to the family center. Governor Keating was also there. We all visited with the counselors beforehand, seeking their guidance on what to say. In that meeting was Victoria Cummock, who flew into Oklahoma City at her own expense to be of assistance to the families while they waited. She could directly relate to the families, as her husband had been killed on Pan Am Flight 101.

Mrs. Cummock stood up and said, "Gentlemen, you tell them the truth. If there is a chance that some people will not be found or there is no chance for survivors at this time, then you tell them. One of the worst things about this time is the not knowing." We took her advice.

Chief Marrs did a good job with the families. He was very serious, very reverent and respectful. He talked about places we had searched as well as places we were having trouble reaching. He talked about the possibility of not finding some of their loved ones in the rubble and the reasons that could happen.

As he continued to detail the situation, I joined in the discussion. We talked about the force of the one-inch plate glass windows as they were shattered by the blast. There were hundreds of thousands of pieces of razor-sharp shrapnel driven through the building at an extremely high rate of speed. There were areas inside the building where glass was imbedded into walls, Sheetrock, chairs, and desks.

Both the chief and I were painfully truthful with these families. Since none of them had been to the building, we had brought pictures so they could see the progress we were making. We showed, to the best of our ability, where offices used to be and what the areas looked like now.

People ask me all the time: what questions did the family members ask you most? And they're always surprised by my answer. Of course people would be curious about how we were doing in terms of procedures and length of time, and they were anxious about the realistic chances of finding survivors. But a lot of their questions were:

"How are *you* doing, Jon?" "How are your men and women holding up?" "How are the law enforcement officers who continue to guard the perimeters?" "How are the FBI and ATF agents doing as they sort through the mess and work to outline steps for the investigation?" It seems they always focused on how rescue workers were doing. They were even concerned about the rescue dogs that were injuring their paws while crawling through the debris. It was always such an uplifting and humbling experience to talk with them. We keyed off their energy and their spirit.

There were reports of incredible escapes to safety immediately following the blast, and some of them were true. We were so focused on getting inside to those who couldn't help themselves that most of us missed the chance to see many of the little miracles that happened. Apparently a local television station reported that one gentleman said he was in his office on the fifth floor one minute and the next he found himself standing outside in the street, unharmed. That story has caused a lot of people to ask me how a person could fall that far and live.

I don't know the specifics of that particular situation, but it's possible that if the floor fell, he rode down with it. Hitting another floor below could have cushioned his fall. As his floor slid out into the street, it moved him out of the way of the floors falling from above. I'm not saying that's what happened. I'm only saying it's possible. Miracles do happen, and everyone at the Alfred P.

Murrah Federal Building who survived the explosion now understands that in the most personal way.

9

Unsung Heroes

HUNDREDS OF THOUSANDS of people watched in horror as the hours following the bombing of the Federal Building showed the nation the very worst of what people can do. Their hearts went out to the families of victims, to the survivors who were robbed of their innocence and their safety, and to the rescuers who toiled for hours inside, searching every inch of the rubble. Then, before anyone had time to ask, Americans began to give of themselves without concern for recognition or the cost of their personal sacrifices.

The goodness and generosity of our city . . . our county . . . our state . . . our nation, was as important to the rescue effort as any one single factor. Constant expressions of love and support, from the smallest to the most extravagant gesture, provided renewed strength for the men and women who were working their way through the destruction.

While rescue workers are deeply grateful for the love and response shown us, it has been very tough for many of those who serve with me to deal with the public perception that we are in some way "heroes." We know that we are simply a group of men and women who had a job to do and we did it. While our task in this case was tougher than most, it was nevertheless our responsibility and our obligation to enter that building to search for and rescue survivors and to recover victims for their families and loved ones. While the world began to call us heroes, we never lost sight of the truth—that the real heroes are the people who gave of themselves freely and out of the goodness of their hearts. They made finishing our job possible and they restored the faith of our nation.

On Thursday, May 11, 1995, I had the honor of accepting a *Newsweek* American Achievement Award on behalf of all the rescuers who participated in the search and rescue effort that followed the horrific bombing of the Alfred P. Murrah Federal Building in Oklahoma City. I was deeply moved by the opportunity to represent every person involved in the effort on that stage at the Kennedy Center in Washington, D.C., and I'd like to share with you what was printed in the program to recognize the contributions of everyone who responded to the challenges presented to us on April 19, and in the days that followed:

. . . The unprecedented rescue effort showed the nation at its bravest and most generous. Literally thousands of police, firefighters, paramedics, federal emergency workers, heavy-rescue specialists, soldiers, structural engineers and ordinary citizens rushed to the scene—and worked round the clock to free the injured and search for survivors. For days on end, these extraordinary men and women braved falling debris—and growing despair—often risking their own safety in the precarious rubble. Hundreds more doctors, nurses, clergy, psychologists and blood donors volunteered as well; schoolchildren from around the world sent messages of hope and condolence. Those efforts helped lift the spirits of the nation in a time of terror—and reassure us all that there is far more heart than hate in the American heartland.

Many of you watched the story unfold on television, in national magazines, and on the front page of virtually every newspaper in the country. In visiting with reporters each day, it was my job to provide a face and a voice for rescuers working in the building. It was important to me, and still is, that you know that I represent the hundreds of firefighters, police officers, and other rescue personnel who were working at the site. It was a privilege to be the person who provided the world with daily information about the rescue mission.

In this chapter I'm asking other people to join me in becoming representatives of what we all experienced following the bombing in Oklahoma City. There were thousands of people who offered their kindness and their support, and those people made their way into the hearts of this nation as "unsung heroes." I'd like you to meet just a few of them now, and ask that you allow them to represent the many, many more who deserve our thanks and appreciation.

A special thanks to . . .

Sharlotte Campbell, for taking a small black spider monkey to play with the children whose relatives were still missing after five days of waiting. Even I had the chance to play with Charlie.

The countless people around this country who lined up and waited hours to give blood when the call went out. People waited eight, nine, ten hours in line to give blood . . . and did it with good spirits.

Our three local TV affiliates and the many radio stations who shared their resources and information with the national media in the early hours of the disaster. The same stations who turned their airways over to rescue teams communicating important information to the public and leading the drives for food, money, and supplies. Their generosity helped reduce the number of curious citizens who made their way to the site in the early critical hours and ensured that the public knew what our needs were at every moment.

The hundreds of people who donated water through a program set up by Eureka Water. Workers were at constant risk of dehydration, but we had all the fluids we needed because citizens called the company to say, "Put it on my tab and take rescuers another bottle of water."

The men and women who work for the city of Oklahoma City. Workers from the Street Department, from water maintenance, water, and waste water, from the Department of Airports, from all the public works departments and health departments. The city manager's clerical staff. The Public Information Office, specifically Karen Farney because she organized the live news conferences at the Civic Center and the Myriad Convention Center so the world could stay informed.

Little Caesar's Pizza for the mobile pizza oven set up right by our main checkpoint. When a rescue worker walked out of the Federal Building for a break, they wouldn't hand him a slice of pizza, they would hand him an entire pizza in a box.

The Center City Post Office, just to the north and west of the building. They handed their building over to us. They offered free stamps and free cards to the rescue workers from out of town so they could keep in touch with loved ones.

Kegy Ruark from Charlie's Barbecue in Vinita, nearly two hundred miles away. He hooked up his cherry-red trailer and brought free beef sandwiches, soda, and chips for people in the area. Though I didn't eat much for the first several days, I do remember that there were dozens like him.

Major David Stevens, one of our station officers, who was assigned to a supply center set up by our maintenance shop in the Journal Record parking garage on the north side of Sixth Street. Staffed by Oklahoma City fire personnel, it became known by all as "Wal-Mart" and Dave—well, he was kind of the Radar O'Reilly, if you know what I mean. If you needed it, Dave would find a way to get it. He either knew who to contact or knew where it was and knew how to make it happen for you—and quick.

Chaplain Ted Wilson of the Oklahoma City Fire Department and Chaplain Jack Poe of the Oklahoma City Police Department. Both men arrived shortly after the first rescuers and they stayed with us until the end. More chaplains came in from all over the country. The FBI chaplain was there. The county sheriff's chaplain was there. Every now and then you would see one of these men in their hard hats which were marked with a cross and the word CHAPLAIN. You could always count on them to come up and give you a big hug. Day by day they lifted our spirits.

These chaplains talked not only with rescue workers, they also talked with volunteers. They talked with the media. They talked to people on the street, those lining up on the other side of the fence, wanting to get a glimpse of the building. They were there to help everybody. Someone told me that there were over seven hundred clergy and chaplains involved in helping people throughout the community, and I believe it. We felt their support.

Oklahoma City Mayor Ron Norick and our city manager, Don Bown, were at the scene very early on, offering the full support of the city, and they were back often, delivering on their promise time and time again. I specifically remember the mayor telling Chief Marrs and me, "Anything you need and it's yours."

Governor and Mrs. Keating, who were at the site every single day, talking with rescuers. They have led fund-raising efforts to ensure that victims' needs will be met.

State Representative Kevin Cox, who set aside concerns for his own safety early on, running to the YMCA to help retrieve children in that day care center. State Representative Chris Hastings, who organized a going-away dinner at the National Cowboy Hall of Fame for all the Urban Search and Rescue teams here from out of town. Lieutenant Governor Mary Fallin, many of our legislators, and every member of the City Council who offered hope and support through personal site visits.

Presbyterian Hospital, who showed up at their own initiative, offering to provide massage services to rescue workers following their shifts in the building. We set them up at the critical stress management areas.

The hairstylists who volunteered their time to give the rescue workers haircuts at the Myriad Convention Center.

The Oklahoma Restaurant Association. Who could say enough about all they did? Countless volunteers always wore a big smile and provided a warm meal. Always.

The Dallas Cowboys. I never was much of a Cowboys fan, though I had a lot of respect for the players. But among the many things that changed as a result of this tragedy is my enthusiasm for the team. They came, seeking no media attention, just to spend time with the rescue workers and volunteers at the site. They brought T-shirts and gimme caps. They signed autographs. They put their arms around rescue workers. They shook hands with everyone they met.

I'll never forget overhearing Troy Aikman, Michael Irvin, and Emmit Smith saying over and over again, "We are the sports figures, you men and women are the heroes. We are here because we look up to you and count it a privilege to be here." They were sincere about everything they said and everything they did. They came to lift the spirits of rescue workers and scored a touchdown with all of us.

I certainly understand now why they call the Dallas Cowboys "America's team."

The First Christian Church, which opened its doors and became a temporary haven for victims' families. The congregation ministered to our city's families in dozens of ways that we'll never know.

The hundreds of people who donated things to make the stay for out-of-state rescue teams a memorable experience. One rescuer told me that he got to the point where he quit asking for something because he would ask for one and ten would show up! Another firefighter told me that his team "wanted for nothing, absolutely nothing." Anytime rescue workers returned to their beds, they were met with cards, candy, teddy bears, flowers, and other expressions of appreciation.

The Daily Oklahoman and Hi-Shots International of Salem, Illinois, for professionalism when allowed inside the perimeter to take pictures. I'll never forget Terry Phillips of Hi-Shots saying his company came to Oklahoma City like everyone else, expecting to be overwhelmed by the tragedy. Instead, they were overwhelmed by the people.

Southwestern Bell Telephone Company. They turned over their entire building at Eighth and Harvey, just three blocks north of the site. Our command post was in their parking lot on the east side. It was a secured area for Oklahoma City police officers to monitor because it had a fence. The Oklahoma Restaurant Association had their food line set up inside. There was also a supply depot where rescuers could get gloves, boots, dry socks, even sweatshirts when it turned cold. There was a makeshift drugstore providing things like aspirin and suntan lotion. There were RNs on duty giving tetanus shots and nonprescription medicines. All this hands-on support by the company who had already agreed to donate one million dollars to the relief fund was truly overwhelming for all of us.

The hundreds of Red Cross and Salvation Army volunteers who performed every request asked of them and met needs before they were asked. Both organizations were incredible and there could never be enough ways or enough time to say thank-you to these angels on earth.

* * *

The Road Bearing Motorcycle Club from Meridian, Mississippi. They presented $500 to the Oklahoma City Fire Department, along with a banner made by the residents of Meridian expressing the town's appreciation to the firefighters.

Oklahoma National Guard Sergeant Larry Medina and his wife, Susan, for caring for the temporary memorials at the site. When the search and rescue operation was completed and the memorials were being removed, the Medinas took some of the items and started a new one in front of the YMCA so there will still be a place for people to leave tokens of their respect.

One day when we were walking back down to the building from our command post, we saw Larry with his daughter, a gorgeous little girl about three years old. He said to her, "Sweetheart, give these guys a hug," and she opened her arms wide. He was not only giving of himself, but he shared his entire family with us.

Cellular One for providing a mobile cell site and much-needed equipment in downtown Oklahoma City within an hour of the blast. Southwestern Bell Mobile Systems brought phones as well. Both companies were unbelievable assets to us, as they enhanced our ability to communicate throughout the entire operation.

* * *

The construction workers and companies who helped us monitor and stabilize the building throughout our search. These men and women often risked their own safety to provide for the safety of rescue workers. They would go first into the most unstable areas and drive steel pipes and wood pilings between broken structures that otherwise might have collapsed on rescue workers. The construction companies gave their resources and materials with no thought of compensation.

The medical examiner's team. They worked feverishly to identify bodies, working around the clock to meet the demands of their gruesome task.

Medical workers and volunteers who raced to the scene and to hospitals to provide medical care to the wounded. We wish we could have found many more survivors and given the medical professionals even more work to do.

Phillip Sternberg, a Vietnam veteran who sent his Purple Heart to honor the children that were killed in the bombing. This man spent three tours of duty in Vietnam and deserved the honor bestowed on him, yet he wanted the families to know that his heart was with them. Sending his medal by way of the Governor, it was displayed at the church where the families were waiting for news of their loved ones.

* * *

School kids from all over the area who came to the Myriad Convention Center during the days following the bombing. Reality was beginning to set in and we were fully aware that time was working against us. The mood in the dining hall was somber and quiet. At least that was the case until the kids descended upon us, bringing cards and hugs to renew our spirits. It wasn't the first time or the last that a group of kids had an impact on rescue workers, but it serves as just one example of the important role that children played throughout the entire mission.

The three million plus Oklahomans who refused to allow this tragedy to break their spirit. They fought back with courage and faith, giving of themselves time and again.

The survivors of the blast. People who thought immediately about their coworkers and other people in the area. Many disregarded their own immediate needs to be of assistance to others. Many have hurdles to cross before they can restore normality to their lives. They have all been changed, but they are embracing the future, and providing inspiration to us all.

Governor Frank Keating and Mayor Ron Norick, two men who, throughout this crisis, showed class, courage, and compassion that should be modeled by every elected official in the country.

* * *

In addition to all these heroes and heroines of the past few weeks, there are four others who unknowingly played an integral role in this incident.

... our department's three fallen firefighters who perished in a 1989 flashover fire in a south Oklahoma City home: Captain Jimmy Ayers, Captain Benny Zellner, and Firefighter Jeff Lindsey.

Their dramatic deaths were the turning point in the campaign to establish a special sales tax for public safety. As a result of this measure, which was strongly supported by our community on election day, our fire and police departments were able to purchase updated equipment and add additional staff. In fact, many of the rescuers on April 19 had been hired as part of that 1989 program. The one-hundred-thirty-five-foot aerial ladder truck, the ninety-five-foot aerial platform, plus other vital equipment that saved lives in this incident had been purchased with money generated by this fund. Though Brian Espe didn't know it at the time, these three men played a key role in his rescue. With coaching from Firefighter Mike Ollman, Mr. Espe crept down the one-hundred-thirty-five-foot aerial ladder as the world watched with a sense of relief.

Yes, Benny, Jeff, and Jimmy were with us ... their spirit was with us. They were and continue to be heroes for this community.

... retired Oklahoma City Fire Chief Tom Smith, who, with the new sales tax funding in 1989, set the stage for innovative equipment purchases and new training standards. Chief Smith implemented our department's Incident Command System, the one used to organize rescue efforts at the Murrah Building.

And the real heroes . . . the families of the 168 people who died. They showed the nation the best that people can be even in the face of tremendous loss. They were always concerned about the safety of the rescue workers, always thanking us and urging the chief and me to keep workers out of harm's way. We fiercely protected their privacy because they deserved at least that from us, but I wish you could have known them like we did. They were incredible people and we will never forget them. They will always hold a special place in each of our hearts.

10

Symbols and Connections

ON SATURDAY, THREE days after the bombing, search and rescue efforts were further aggravated by cold winds and rain. Twice that morning our rescue efforts were delayed. Standing in the freezing rain, we all felt frustrated and helpless. We had so much to do, such hopes for what we could accomplish, and it seemed like everything was working against us. As much as we felt driven to move ahead, the building couldn't tolerate the conditions. We needed something to lift our spirits. And typical of this operation, because we needed something, it came.

One of our firefighters brought me a little red fire truck he had found inside in the day care area. Ravaged and broken, it still brought a smile to my face. I could imagine one of the children in the center playing with it, perhaps pretending to be a firefighter.

And now, here we were, tackling obstacle after obstacle, hoping to save a child's life . . . to give him a chance to join us at Firehouse No. 1. The odds were against us both, but the truck reminded us that we couldn't give up. We had to keep trying.

I carried the little fire engine up to the press area to show them what we'd found. I'll never forget that interview, standing in the rain, clutching that familiar object that had been pulled from the rubble. I told the press that day, "The firefighters inside the building asked me to bring this truck out here to show you. They want the world to know that this broken toy is a symbol of our broken hearts."

People commented to me about that story over and over again—about how much it meant to them. A picture of me holding the truck made it into newspapers all across this country. I realized something important then. Clearly, people wanted to identify personally with the story we were telling them. They were able to respond to symbols because it gave them something tangible to grasp hold of when nothing around us made sense.

After that I began to watch for other things that would help us summarize and express what we were experiencing. Understanding what people needed helped me tell the story in ways that were more personal and they could understand. And there was another dimension to all of this as well.

Once we knew it was a bomb that had wreaked this havoc on the Federal Building, we were confused about what kind of person could commit this kind of terrorist act. And I've learned that when things around you look strange and confused, hanging on to something familiar can make all the difference in the world. While the men inside the building were searching for victims, I began to search for better ways to help the public understand what was happening to us all.

It was early in the recovery effort that a tattered and torn American flag was brought from the building and presented to the Governor. I'll never again look at our country's flag without remembering the courage it represents—rescue workers risking their lives to find survivors and to deliver loved ones to waiting relatives. Family members who were facing the greatest nightmare of their lives finding the courage to show the world a dignity and grace we didn't expect.

As the Governor was accepting the flag, my immediate thought was about the Pledge of Allegiance that we all learn as children. "One nation, under God, indivisible, with liberty and justice for all." I'll always remember the people who tried to destroy our faith with a bomb, and the way this country responded. When times were tough, we pulled together, and showed the world we are truly one nation.

* * *

There's another symbol of greatness that many of us always knew, but the rest of the world just learned about it. It's the symbol of our great state, the state of Oklahoma. Over sixteen days, the world watched our citizens respond to the tragedy that blew our lives apart, and quickly they began to see us as the heart of the nation. The Heartland is what they called us. And it's a nickname that fits.

Throughout the incident I talked with reporters from coast to coast and I discovered that people see Oklahoma differently now. The place we call home is now a place others want to visit. It's now a place where people say they would be proud to live. Nothing's changed in Oklahoma, but something's changed *for* Oklahoma. The world has seen us for who we are and we've set a new standard for what a state can be.

Early on it never occurred to me that people would want pieces of the building that housed the greatest terror we've ever known. The fact that something like this could happen in a place like Oklahoma was almost more than we could bear. I thought that the building itself would always remind us of the innocence that was stolen from us.

But over time, surprisingly enough, the building ceased to be something we were afraid of and became a reminder that the power of good is stronger than the power of evil. We will never forget the people who lost their lives there, but we will add to that memory the way this entire country pulled together to show that we would not be defeated. We refused to let the people who lost their lives die in vain. They would call us all to reach inside ourselves and to offer up the best we could be.

When I think about that building, even today, there are things that I want to forget, but there is so much more I want to remember. I plan to remember the way this community, this state, and this nation—indeed, thousands of people from around the world—responded to this crisis from the bottoms of their hearts.

So people began wanting a piece of the ravaged building. . . . And I guess when you stop and think about it, who can blame them? It's not a morbid souvenir they were after, but a reminder of the spirit and compassion that helped us survive the worst disaster we've ever known.

For many, the rescue workers themselves became symbols of what is right and brave in America. People call us heroes. Powerful symbols of assertive response. Even when the risk was great, our firefighters, police officers, and others stepped forward and did their jobs. Brave? Definitely. Selfless? Without a doubt. Heroes? If heroes are those who are willing to give their lives for others, then the title fits the people who worked day and night in the shifting Murrah Building.

* * *

Since I was a child, and maybe before that, Billy Graham has been one of the symbols of religion in this country. He has ministered to our nation and counseled presidents of both political parties. When he came to Oklahoma, he proved why he's a man who has earned the respect of millions, and why Oklahoma needed him here for the memorial service held the Sunday following the explosion.

Rescue workers didn't get to attend the whole service, but later I heard about what he had to say. At a time when none of us had the right answers about what was happening in our state, Billy Graham came and asked the right question: "Why would God let this happen?" He asked the question that all of us are afraid to ask because we're equally afraid of the answer. Only Billy Graham would have the courage to ask the question. Only Billy Graham would have the courage to answer it with the truth: "I don't know why."

At the end of the first day I was absolutely exhausted. On top of everything else, the weight of my helmet was wearing me out. It was hot and heavy, and I knew right away that I needed an alternative. I remembered that my softball cap was in the car—the one that says OKLA CITY FIRE on the front—and I knew that it was the solution I was searching for.

When I first started wearing the hat, reporters didn't say much, but over time it became an important part of the visual effect they were looking

for. I liked wearing it because for me it represented the team spirit of all the agencies and
groups that had pulled together to meet this
challenge. This was certainly no game we were
playing, but all the things that make a softball
team successful were at work here: training, tal-
ent, teamwork, and a little bit of luck. Each and
every day, as I went to the command post, as I
walked through the building, I couldn't help but
say to myself, "This is truly a team I'm proud to
be a part of."

Tears flowed freely at the Federal Building, as
there were many reasons to cry. But the best reason of all, many never stopped to think about. It
just happened. Tears became a symbol of being
real . . . of being strong. There were many times
when I'd see a rescue worker wiping away a tear,
and frankly I was glad. That building made us
deal with the worst of humanity and you had to
tear up to keep from tearing up.

I was glad to see rescuers cry because that
meant we would survive this ordeal and come
out whole. Though we are trained to set our
emotions aside and focus on the task in front of
us, the raw pain we felt as we moved through
that building demanded our humanity as well as
our professionalism.

Captain Chris Fields is a guy who was just doing
his job, and suddenly he became a national symbol of the rescue effort in Oklahoma City. Baylee

Almon, a young child in the America's Kids Day Care Center, found her way to his arms when a police officer delivered her from the building. An amateur photographer standing nearby snapped a riveting photo, and the picture ended up in newspapers throughout the world.

When Chris woke up and saw his picture in the paper, initially he had a hard time dealing with it. He knew that he was one of several rescue workers, part of a human chain that played a role in getting Baylee out of the building, and he didn't want people to falsely assume that he had acted alone. He didn't want Police Sergeant John Avera to be overlooked in the rescue attempt, because he had played an equal or greater role.

One of the concepts we pay a lot of attention to at the fire department is teamwork, and Chris is in every way a team player. It took more than one conversation with Chris to help him believe that while people see him as a symbol of what happened on April 19, they aren't trying to separate him from the rest of the people he serves with. Frankly, it was a little refreshing to find someone resisting the spotlight instead of seeking it. It makes sense that that someone was Chris Fields.

Almost from the moment the bomb exploded, citizens were searching for ways to respond. They wanted desperately to do something to help. They wanted to show the world that they were watching and hoping.

I'm not sure how it began or what the purpose was. Jenifer tells me people just started calling the television station. By the weekend, word had spread asking citizens to turn their car lights on as an expression of support for the victims and the rescuers. For days and days you couldn't drive anywhere in Oklahoma City, even in the middle of the day, without seeing almost every single car with its headlights on.

I wasn't away from the site much, but a lot of people told me about the car lights. It seemed like a good idea to me, as our world was in such dire need of a little encouragement. People with their car lights on sat side by side at intersections, passed one another without saying a word. No words were needed because the lights said it all: we're in this together.

It seemed like a small matter when they brought it up; Governor Keating and Mayor Norick decided to call for a moment of silence on the one-week anniversary of the bombing at 9:02 A.M. I guess it was a little thing that got a big response. People were pulling off the road, stopping conversations, stopping every activity imaginable. President Clinton stopped. The State Legislature stopped. The rescuers stopped. For that one moment the hectic schedules we allow to rule our lives came to a stop. It was one of the few times when the world acted in accord.

* * *

I think it started the day the bomb exploded. People began talking about whether or not the building should be taken down and rebuilt. Those who thought a memorial should be placed on the site began formulating what kind of memorial should be built so that we would always remember April 19, 1995: what we lost . . . what we found . . . what we accomplished in the weeks that followed.

There has never been any doubt in anyone's mind that there would be a memorial. The only questions have been: What will it be? To whom will it pay tribute? Who will make the decision?

We will always remember April 19. Not only will we remember the day, we'll remember what happened. Not only will we remember what happened, we'll remember exactly where we were at 9:02 A.M., when the bomb went off. Just as clearly and as certainly as we remember where we were the moment President Kennedy was shot.

Love comes in many colors. Just ask the Oklahomans who wore ribbons on their clothes throughout the rescue operation. There was no official declaration to do it. Again, regular Oklahomans just set out to show their support, and that's exactly what happened.

Ribbons showed up on lapels in numerous colors, all unique in design. Schools, shops, charities, businesses—all had original creations that meant something special to the people who made them. Eventually, *The Daily Oklahoman* printed a color chart, more because people were asking for guidance than to coordinate the activity.

Yellow . . . hope for those still missing
Blue . . . for the state of Oklahoma
White . . . for the innocence of the victims
Purple . . . for the courage of the children
Green . . . for prayers for the victims
Red, white, and blue . . . for united support

Oklahomans proved again and again by their spontaneous creations what all of us had hoped is true—that some emotions simply come straight from the heart.

11

Gone But Not Forgotten

A T 5:45 A.M., on Tuesday, May 23, Jim Denny and I were standing together downtown, waiting to be interviewed by *CBS Morning News*. The sun was rising behind us, and I smiled as I remembered their theme song, "Oh, What a Beautiful Morning" from the musical *Oklahoma!*

We talked about what was happening in our lives while we waited to talk to Paula Zahn about the implosion of the Alfred P. Murrah Federal Building scheduled for 7:00 A.M. I was honored to be there with Jim as he's one of the true heroes in the Oklahoma City bombing story. On April 19, Jim and his wife had two children in the America's Kids Day Care Center. Miraculously, both survived, but they spent weeks in area hospitals recovering from blast injuries.

We were both ready for the building to come down. It was time.

I'll have to admit I was feeling emotional about it. Rescuers had lived our lives there for sixteen days straight. We'd been over every inch of the building on numerous occasions, with the exception of one small area we couldn't reach. Our lives had been on hold while we worked around the clock searching through debris of concrete and steel for the remains of human life and hope.

It had been several days since the end of the search and rescue effort. We'd been working hard, long hours every day, to get back to the routine of life, though it had hardly been life as usual. Between professional responsibilities and personal obligations, days had been full for rescuers. There were and continue to be a whole list of thank-yous to be said.

Following our conversation with CBS, I left Jim and proceeded to the media area to do several more interviews. I continued talking with reporters until about twenty minutes to seven when I had to leave for the Regency Tower apartment complex where I was scheduled to watch the implosion.

Security was extremely tight. Law enforcement officers surrounded the perimeter so that they could keep the public back and safe. Mac Maguire, the contractor managing the rebuilding of the Regency Tower, met me on the ground floor and welcomed me into the building.

My position to watch the implosion was on the fifteenth floor, so I got on the elevator and was escorted up by security guards. When we reached my stop, I found Mayor Ron Norick, fire department photographer Danny Ashley, Major Rick Williams (who had been my right arm throughout the entire incident), Sergeant Avera of the Oklahoma City Police Department, and a couple of sheriff's deputies. Then, to my surprise, I caught a glimpse of the family members of the two victims still missing—the Thompson family and Debbie and Bob Pippin, the parents of Christy Rosas. What a privilege to be selected to watch the building come down with them.

There was a large window where we could all look out, and we were very respectful of each other. There was plenty of room. I even set up my personal video camera on a tripod in a corner of the window, letting it run so that it would capture the building's collapse.

Right on time we heard the systematic warnings start . . . followed by a long final blast. As soon as the last one sounded, dynamite in the building started to explode. Though people later would tell me that the implosion happened quickly, at the time it seemed like it took an eternity for the building to go down. It didn't—it was only eight seconds.

The implosion was not only fast, but it was also very loud. Frankly, I didn't expect that. In other implosions I've witnessed, the noise has always been very muffled. But there was a difference in all those cases, the damage was always contained inside the buildings that were coming down. In this case, the jagged Murrah Building was blown open, providing no buffer for the sound. I think the loudness of it shocked a lot of people. I know it shocked me.

First, the center of the building collapsed, then the east side, then the west. Finally, as planned, a huge elevator and stairway shaft toppled over, adding to the heaping pile of new rubble. Gray smoke clouds arose from the ground, dust was making the sky hazy. As the building came down, a lot of emotions came up.

None of us in the room said much. Phillip, Mrs. Thompson's son, spoke for all of our pain when he said simply, "Goodbye, Mom." There wasn't anything else to say. We just stood there for about five to ten minutes waiting for the dust to completely clear. We had a good view of the building, now blown into pieces, ready to be hauled off. Looking at that mountain of rubble I could not help but think about the broken lives the April 19 bombing had caused. The time it would take to haul off the new pile of debris would be nothing compared to how long we would all need to put our lives back together.

Regardless of how the rest of the world felt, the two families we were with were glad to see the building down because it was a necessary step before we could go back into that one unsearched area to try to locate their loved ones. If only for that reason, and there were many others, I was glad the deed was finally done.

Before we left, Mr. Pippin asked me if he could

have my Oklahoma City Fire ball cap—the one I wore that first day. He didn't want the one I had on right then—with DISASTER IN THE HEARTLAND, APRIL 19, 1995 embroidered on the back. He wanted the one that I actually wore during the incident which said FIRE RESCUE. Christy Rosas had a five-year-old son named Shane, and they wanted that hat to go to him. I felt honored that they asked and glad I had something I could give to a small boy who had so much taken away.

We walked out of the building together, promising to make it a priority to stay in touch. As we exchanged phone numbers, the families got into the van that was waiting to take them back to their cars outside the perimeter. I took a couple of pictures from ground level, thanked Mr. Maguire for his hospitality, and drove back to the media area where I had a number of interviews scheduled. Reporters wanted to know what it was like for me to stand in front of the bombed-out shell where I'd done hundreds of media interviews over the past several weeks. That was easy. I felt like we had all just taken a step in the healing process. Not that our community wouldn't still have much to deal with as we struggled through the long-term aftershocks of this horrific tragedy—but it was a start.

When it was all said and done, I guess it was about noon. It would be days before enough debris would be removed so that we could recover the missing victims. As I headed back to my office five blocks away, I realized that those of us in

Oklahoma City would always feel differently about bombings in other countries. We would never again pass casually over an article in the newspaper about devastation somewhere else. From now on, we would always know in a very personal way that brutality has innocent victims. The building in Oklahoma City that had its heart torn out changed everything for us.

That afternoon, I continued to work with firefighters on documenting everything that happened in our rescue and recovery effort. Throughout the department there is interest in becoming a FEMA/USAR team. We know that we owe this country a lot for the help that was so willingly given to us. And because of the experiences we had when the worst of humanity blew our lives apart, we now have expertise that might some day be of use to some other city in crisis.

Within our community, we work daily to heal our torn hearts and to keep our spirits up. There are memorial services and appreciation ceremonies happening almost daily. Firefighters, like other rescue workers, are spending a lot of time saying thank you to the people, and especially the children, who sent us posters, cards, cookies, and dozens of other expressions of support.

This is a time for giving thanks, for remembering back to the blur of those days to see example after example of the ways people can come together when dealt life's worst. I find myself remembering things now that I didn't even notice at the time, and it gives me all the more reason to feel grateful. I'll give you an example.

We weren't too far into the rescue and recovery effort when Chief Marrs asked me if my wife Jenifer had been down to the site. I didn't think much about the question because I assumed he was wondering if she had been downtown for her station, reporting on daily events. I told him that she hadn't been, at least not that I was aware of. It slipped my mind after that, and it wasn't until much later when I was talking to Jenifer one night at home that I thought of it again.

We were talking about the building and some of the things that were happening at the site. It was a good release for me to be able to talk to her, and it was easy because she knew a lot about what was happening. She'd been reporting the story to her viewers from day one. I don't remember exactly what I was referring to, but I do remember saying that "you would almost have to have been down there to know what I'm talking about."

Jenifer surprised me by saying simply, "I've been there." I found out she hadn't gone for her job. Her job was at the anchor desk. She'd visited the site because she's my wife and she wanted to see and understand what I was going through. I never saw her because she couldn't get inside the perimeter.

Since the rescue effort has ended and I've had a chance to talk with some of the people who served down there with me every day, I've

learned that many of the rescuers' wives and
family members found their way downtown because they wanted to know personally something
about the things we were experiencing. They
knew that we'd all be living with the memories
for a long time to come.

Quiet support. I'm beginning to suspect that
those of us who were there will never know just
how much so many did to help us all survive the
nightmare we lived in the Alfred P. Murrah Federal Building.

I've been back to the building a number of
times since the implosion. Being responsible for
our department's special operations and being
the department's spokesman, I have to go back
for meetings about what steps will be taken next.
It feels different to go there now, partially because it looks so different. The now three-story-
high rubble is far less intimidating than the
nine-story building that used to tower over us.
The place where rescuers lived the nightmare is
gone. And, in another two and a half weeks, all
the debris will be removed, and there will be
grass planted on that corner that captured the attention of this entire country for weeks. For good
or bad, we'll be left to deal with the memories in
places that will only exist somewhere inside ourselves.

Luckily, there are a lot of us who will be dealing with the memories, and just like was true
throughout the incident, we will have one another. From the first moment, this effort was

about "we" and not "I." It was about dozens of public safety agencies pulling together. It was about lots and lots of people doing their jobs. It was about hundreds more doing things that weren't their jobs; instead their actions were an outpouring of the faith and love that lies within the people of this great nation. It was about family members who let us all embrace them as we struggled through our pain. This has always been about all of us.

One of the good things about having to "get back to normal" is that life really calls you back. In my case I have budgets to deal with, papers on my desk that have been piling up for weeks, a family who loves me and has been patiently waiting for some of my time. There are still issues related to the bombing to be addressed and public appearances to be made throughout the community. Thanks to a wonderful staff, we're prioritizing everything and moving forward.

The rest of the nation may heal before we do in Oklahoma City. We still drive by the 200 block of Northwest Fifth Street, a place that will always be a reminder of this senseless tragedy. We don't have to close our eyes to remember the victims because we will see their families and their friends as part of our living life in this community. We won't cease to feel the support of the countless hours spent by volunteers because this community has become a family.

It's hard to know what the future holds. Some very bad people reminded us all that something can happen at any moment to change our lives forever. And these days my schedule is so hectic that I sometimes meet myself coming and going. Plans are changing all the time to meet the needs of the day. There is so much to be done that I'm finding it hard to say with certainty what I'll be doing beyond next week.

But there's one date circled on my calendar in red, one date that I need no calendar to remember: April 19. In a life full of uncertainty, one thing I know for sure—next year, God willing, on April 19, at 9:02 A.M., I will be in the 200 block of Northwest Fifth Street paying tribute to those who lost their lives. I'll be paying tribute to those families who have survived even though they lost so much. I'll be paying tribute to the people of this city, this state, this nation, for the countless ways they contributed to our belief in the future when the reality of the present was really tough to handle. I'll be paying tribute to the hundreds of rescue workers who helped the world pull together as it watched people do their jobs with a tremendous respect for human life.

For sixteen days straight, I had the responsibility of telling the world the story about what was happening in downtown Oklahoma City as a result of the worst terrorist act in our country's history. I look forward to spending the rest of my life telling anyone who will listen how the people in this state and nation stood by Oklahoma City. Together we made it through the heartbreak that we experienced in the Heartland.

12

An Update

ON MONDAY, MAY 29, 1995, the bodies of the last three known victims of the April 19 bombing were uncovered in the demolished remains of the Alfred P. Murrah Federal Building. Christy Rosas, twenty-two, and Virginia Thompson, fifty-six, both Credit Union employees, were found about 4:45 P.M. Alvin Justes, a frequent Credit Union customer, was found approximately thirty minutes later. Mr. Justes had been reported missing only a few days before, so we had not included him in earlier "missing" numbers.

The bodies were found exactly where we expected them to be—in the only pile of rubble rescue workers couldn't search earlier due to the structural problems before the building was imploded. Firefighters joined the entire community in expressing a sigh of relief that all victims were finally returned to their families.

The final death toll from this bombing, the most fatal terrorist act in our nation's history, now stands at 168.

Epilogue

THE APRIL 19, 1995, bombing of the Alfred P. Murrah Federal Building took the lives of 168 people. They had no choice in whether or not they would become victims of this tragedy. Someone else made that decision for them.

Those who survived the blast, those who were in the building, and those of us left to deal with the destruction it caused were given another chance at life. We've been given the chance to re-evaluate what's important and to become better people because of what we've been through.

Many people impacted our lives throughout this ordeal, but for those of us who survived, none more than Victoria Cummock, herself a widow of a terrorist act. She brought words of wisdom to the families of the victims, and her insights ended up being a challenge for us all.

In words much more eloquent than mine, she

told us to remember that the victims should only be those who died in the building, just like the people who had died on Pan Am Flight 101 with her husband. The victims are the people who had no choice in their future. She encouraged all of us to give ourselves permission to be survivors, telling us that allowing ourselves to become victims only makes the penetration of this devastation even more ravaging. She challenged us not to let the terrorists add more names to their casualty list by allowing them to make victims of us as well.

Many died here in Oklahoma City on April 19, but we are left living. There are miraculous stories of many who survived the blast and of heroic recoveries. There are stories of the grace and honor displayed by family members and people in our community. There are stories of people who fought back, who said we will not allow these terrorists to rob us of our heart and spirit. I wish I'd had time to tell them all. I wish I'd known them all to tell.

What I do know is that for weeks and years to come, we will live with the impact that this day had on our lives. We will have to deal with the reality that terrible things happen, and they sometimes happen to good, defenseless people. But fortunately, for those who live in Oklahoma City, and for those who watched this disaster from afar, we all also learned that the darkness isn't quite as scary when you have someone with you to hold your hand.

Now, for those who have overcome so much, the challenge to be survivors continues. We must hold on to the national kinship forged in the heat of crisis. To do so would be the highest possible tribute to those injured and killed on April 19, 1995, and to those who risked their lives in the Oklahoma rescue.

Appendix

THROUGHOUT THIS BOOK you've seen the courage and dedication of the men and women of the Oklahoma City Fire Department. I mentioned early on that I couldn't begin to name the individual firefighters who played a significant role in the Alfred P. Murrah Federal Building disaster unless I could name them all.

Ballantine Books and I have therefore decided to cite each and every one of them. These public servants all played an important role in the search and rescue effort, showing concern and compassion for the relatives and loved ones of those whose lives were being slowly torn apart.

I count it as one of the greatest privileges of my life to serve the city of Oklahoma City with this incredible group of people.

OKLAHOMA RESCUE

THE MEN AND WOMEN OF THE OKLAHOMA CITY FIRE DEPARTMENT

PATRICK L. ABBANANTO

A. STEVE ABBOTT

HOWARD W. ADAMS

KENNETH D. ADAMS

KENNY D. ADAMS

MICHAEL R. ADAMS

TIMOTHY R. ADAMS

SHELBY T. ADCOCK

JERALD R. ADUDDELL

PAUL J. AKINS

BRUCE W. ALEXANDER

ROBERT R. ALEXANDER

LARRY L. ALLEN

TOMMY L. ALLEN

CLIFF L. ANDERSEN

MICHAEL ANDERSON

ROY L. ANDREW, JR.

PAUL R. ANKENMAN

ERIC V. ANKNEY

KENNETH R. ANNESLEY

SCOTT L. ANNESLEY

JOHN M. ARCHER

PAUL D. ARCHER

OLEN W. ARDERY, JR.

MARK WAYNE ARGO

BARBARA ARMSTRONG

CLAUD M. ARMSTRONG

BRIAN D. ARNOLD

GARY L. ASHCRAFT

DANNY T. ATCHLEY
LONNIE R. AUSTIN
CARL A. AUTRY
JAMES W. AVANT, JR.
STEVE J. BAGGS
TONY L. BAIRD
DAVID L. BAKER
JACK E. BAKER
GLENN M. BALLINGER
WILLIAM L. BAMBERG
ALLEN J. BARBER
PHILLIP E. BARGMAN
MAX D. BARNES
STEPHEN D. BARNES
JIMMY W. BARNETT
DANIEL L. BARTON
KYLE D. BARTON
MICHAEL L. BATTLES
RODNEY A. BATY
JEFFREY T. BAUGUS
CHARLEY E. BAXTER
MONTE L. BAXTER
JIMMY R. BEAVER
LYNN D. BECK
BILL R. BELCHER
CHRISTOPHER D. BELL
CLAYTON E. BELL
RICHARD T. BELL
ANDY BENNETT
TIMOTHY S. BENNETT
WILLARD J. BENNETT
ALAN BENSON

JAMES F. BEREND
RODNEY A. BEREND
ROBERT W. BERKENBILE
JOHN K. BERRY
RONALD J. BERRY
ROBERT J. BILLEG
MICHAEL E. BISHARD
LOYD J. BISHOP, JR.
TY W. BIVENS
CHRISTOPHER A. BLACK
ERIC E. BLACK
JON M. BLACK
WALTER H. BLACK, JR.
GARY E. BLEHM
JAMES A. BLOCKER
LARRY G. BOATMAN
HOBERT L. BOGGS
BRUCE E. BOLIN
MICHAEL J. BOOTH
NORMAN L. BORDERS
ROGER D. BOREN
THOMAS R. BOREN
DONALD G. BOURASSA
CARL D. BOWERMAN
DAVID F. BOWMAN
JERRY C. BOWMAN
DAVID C. BOYD
THURMAN J. BOYD
DAVID BRADBURY
SHAWN G. BRAY
BRYCE L. BRENT
IVORY O. BRENT

COREY W. BRITT
ROGER D. BROCK
SHAWN H. BROOKS
RYAN B. BROTHERTON
KAREN S. BROWN
RAYMOND M. BROWN
RONNIE BROWN
TERRY L. BROWN
TODD E. BROWN
WILLIAM H. BROWN
MICHAEL J. BRUEHL
PAUL B. BRUM
WENDAL D. BRUNK
JERRY W. BRYAN
BRENT BRYANT
GERALD K. BRYANT
ROBERT M. BUCKNER
KENNETH P. BUNCH
TROY D. BUNCH
CLYDE B. BUNDAGE
KEVIN H. BURGE
RUSSELL R. BURKHALTER
WYATT A. BURKS
MICHAEL T. BURNER
LYLE A. BURRIS
MICHAEL S. BURRIS
ROCKY J. BURT
WILLIAM E. BUTLER
WITEK K. BYCKO
JAMES A. CALDWELL
JOHN M. CALHOON
FRED K. CALHOUN

RICHARD D. CALVERT
D. C. CANTRELL
DANNY C. CAPPS
RONNIE W. CAPPS
STEVEN D. CAPPS
ANTONIO L. CARBAJAL
GERALD F. CARLILE
THOMAS R. CARPENTER
JAMES D. CARR
MATTHEW B. CARTER
RICHARD K. CARTER
SHERMAN M. CARTHEN
CHARLES W. CARTLEDGE, III
BRYON G. CASS
JERRY W. CATLETT
JOE R. CATRON
GUADALUPE CAVAZOS
TODD L. CHAPMAN
PHILLIP CHEATHAM
STEPHEN G. CHEATWOOD
BENNIE D. CHILDRESS
DONALD CHISM, JR.
TIMOTHY S. CHISM
WESLEY D. CHOATE
GAYLE D. CLARK
GLENN A. CLARK
KELLY B. CLARK
CHET W. CLARK
CECIL W. CLAY
TED A. CLAYPOOL
STEPHEN E. CLEMENT
PERRY L. CLOGSTON

DANNY W. CLYMER
CARL G. COBB
MARK A. COCHELL
JERRY B. COFFEY
MICHAEL W. COKER
ROBERT L. COLBERT
ROBIN S. COLBERT
KENT A. COLLINS
CORBIN COLSON
KEVIN L. COLWELL
JAMES L. CONNER
JON J. COOK
KENNETH A. COOK
LONNIE R. COOK
STEPHEN P. COOKE
RUSSELL F. COON
PAUL W. COOPER
CRIS L. COPELAND
GARY L. COPELAND
RAYMOND F. COPPEDGE
ALVIN E. COPS
CLIFFORD E. COPS, JR.
DONALD E. CORNELIUS
RANDY L. CORNELIUS
WILLIE CORNELIUS
MARK L. CORVIN
ALBERT W. COTHRAN
SCOTT A. COTTON
JUSTIN L. COTTRELL
JOHN W. COUNCIL
JEFFERY D. COURTNEY
RICHARD L. COX

TODD L. COX
THOMAS W. CRAUTHERS
RALPH A. CRAWFORD
JON R. CREWS
ROBERT E. CRISP
RONALD G. CRON
JAMES D. CRUMP
NEAL CRUTCHFIELD
CLIFF T. CULP
JOSEPH M. CULP
LUTHER G. CUMMINGS
RON S. CUNNINGHAM
WENDELL C. CUNNINGHAM, II
MYRL J. CUPPY, III
TOMMY L. CURRY
GARY D. CURTIS
TODD A. CUSTER
CURTIS DAILY
DAVID E. DALLAS
KENNETH S. DALLAS
JOHN W. DANIEL
SAMMY R. DAUGHERTY
RODNEY C. DAVENPORT
DARREN S. DAVIDSON
KEVIN L. DAVIDSON
BILLY J. DAVIS
DOUGLAS P. DAVIS
GARY L. DAVIS
JAY K. DAVIS
JIMMY D. DAVIS
MARK A. DAVIS
ROBERT DAVIS

SCOT M. DAVIS
STEPHEN C. DAVIS
TONY J. DAVIS
RALPH A. DAVISON
LORENCE A. DEATON
PAUL R. DEAVER
STEVEN R. DELK
MARK S. DELONG
TRICIA K. DIAZ
ROBERT W. DIBRELL
CHRISTOPHER A. DILL
MARK A. DILLON
RICHARD K. DILLON
KEMPER W. DITZLER
DENNIS L. DOBBS
MARK D. DOBBS
CARL D. DONEVIN
SHELDON DOOLIN
DWAYNE E. DOOLITTLE
MARCUS C. DORSEY
GARY D. DOTY
KENNETH R. DOUGLAS
CURTIS A. DRISCOLL
LATHAN S. DUNCAN
BRAD K. DUNLAP
STEVEN W. DUNN
MARSHALL T. DUNNAM
BARRY K. DURHAM
TROY DYCUS
TERRY K. EDGE
JACKIE W. EDMONSON
MARK S. EDWARDS

ROBERT L. EDWARDS, JR.
STUART R. ELDRIDGE
DENNIS W. ELLIOTT
REUBEN O. ELLIS
JAMES G. ELLZEY
MARK D. ELMORE
RANDAL D. ELMORE
JOHN D. ERICKSON
WILLIAM D. ERWIN
JOHN S. ESPOSITO
MARCUS L. EVANS
BART T. EVERETT
CHAD W. EVERETT
VANCE W. EVERETT, JR.
DAVID L. EWOLDT
HAROLD L. FACTORY
TIMOTHY D. FARMER
LISA FARRIS
EVAN K. FENTON
MARK G. FIELDER
CHRISTOPHER FIELDS
DAVID J. FIELDS
LARRY C. FINCH
DEAN A. FINDLEY
BILLY D. FINN
STEVEN L. FITZGERALD
MICHAEL L. FLEMING
CRAIG A. FLETCHER
ERVIN R. FLETCHER
MIKE FLETCHER
FREDDIE M. FLOWERS
TERESA (TESS) FOLKERS

DONALD FONZI
TERRY L. FONZI
PAUL L. FORD
STEPHEN D. FORSHEE
JAMES W. FOSHEE
MICHAEL J. FOSTER
PHILLIP W. FOSTER
LESLIE FOUGHTY
BOBBY J. FREEMAN
EUGENE D. FREEMAN
JOHNNY W. FREEMAN
CURTIS L. FROH
ELDON S. FULLERTON
RICHARD G. FULTON
WILLIAM D. FULTON
BILLY L. GAINES
LEONARD CHARLES GAINES
RICHARD C. GARDNER
MICHUAL J. GARRETTE
STEVE A. GARRETTE
BRYANT W. GASSETT
LESLIE GAY
CHRISTOPHER E. GELVEN
MICHAEL W. GIBSON
GEORGE W. GIDEON
JESSIE G. GILMORE
CATHY GINTER
HERMAN C. GLOVER
SAMUEL L. GODWIN
GREGORY P. GOFF
TIMOTHY L. GOFF
BRUCE D. GOMEZ

OKLAHOMA RESCUE

LESLIE R. GOMEZ
BRUCE E. GONZALES
DANNY K. GONZALES
RANDY GONZALES
WAYNE C. GOODGION
RALPH M. GOODMAN
JERRY L. GOODRICH
CHRISTOPHER D. GOODWIN
CHARLES R. GORMAN
MICHAEL J. GOURLEY
DAVID R. GRAHAM
NIKKI J. GRAHAM
CURTIS GRAMLING
PHILO R. GRAVITT
CHRISTOPHER R. GRAY
TERRI J. GREENAN
JAMES B. GREENHOWARD, III
OTIS J. GREENHOWARD
CHANNON R. GREENWOOD
CLINTON G. GREENWOOD
STEVE GRELLNER
DENNIS E. GRIFFIN
TRAVIS R. GRIFFIN
ALVIE E. GROVES
KYNDAL HADLOCK
LYNDAL A. HADLOCK
DANNY C. HAGUE
GEORGE H. HALE
MARVIN D. HALL
WILLIAM H. HALLMAN
KEITH R. HAMBURGER
ROBERT D. HAMMER

JAMES H. HAMMOCK, JR.
JIMMY D. HANEY
CHARLES L. HANSEN
JOHN HANSEN, JR.
STEVEN M. HANSEN
MELVIN Y. HANSON, JR.
MICHAEL A. HARDY
DAVID HARLAND
JOHN R. HARPER, III
MICHAEL R. HARPER
KEITH A. HARRIS
RICKY L. HARRIS
SHERI HARRIS
MARK W. HART
TERRY L. HARVEY
MAHLON J. HARVILLE
TIMMIE J. HATAWAY
KIRK D. HAWKINS
GREG A. HAYES
LEO HAYES
SHEILA D. HAYS
GREGORY S. HEARD
JEFF S. HEINZIG
BRYAN HEIRSTON
ERIC HELMS
GARYL B. HENDERSON
HOWARD B. HENDERSON
LOUIS E. HENDERSON
TONY HENSLEY
RICKY G. HENSON
DAVID A. HERMAN
RICKEY F. HERRINGTON

KELLY D. HILBURN
ALLEN L. HILL
CALVIN C. HILL
DAVID K. HILL
CHRIS HOFFMAN
NICK R. HOLLADAY
JERRY D. HOLLINGSWORTH
MAURICE D. HOLLOWAY
KENNETH HOLMAN
PATRICK G. HOPKINS
CHRIS A. HOPPES
MICHAEL D. HORN
JAMES E. HORNE
RICK D. HORNER
VANDON R. HOTTLE
EUGENE A. HOUCK
RAYMOND L. HOUSTON
STEPHEN N. HOWARD
MORRIS G. HOWELL
GREGORY W. HOYLE
RUSSELL G. HUBBARD
JIMMY W. HUDSON
TERRY D. HUDSON
RONALD N. HUFF
RODNEY C. HUSTON
THOMAS E. IAGO
DAVID E. IMHOFF
GEORGE F. IMHOFF
FRANK L. ISAAC
CHRIS A. JACKSON
EDDIE D. JACKSON
KEVIN G. JACKSON

MICHAEL D. JACKSON
RICHARD H. JACKSON
ROBERT B. JACKSON
MICHAEL J. JAMES
RONALD D. JARRETT
CHARLES M. JAY, JR.
JOY L. JEFFERSON
ROBERT C. JENNER
JOSEPH E. JOHNS
DONALD R. JOHNSON
JEFFREY D. JOHNSON
GARRY L. JONES
HOMER E. JONES
J. MIKE JONES
MICHAEL C. JONES
RUDOLPH R. JONES
WILLIAM A. JUSTICE
RONNIE D. KEE
MICHAEL D. KEETON
PAUL V. KEETON, JR.
MARK S. KEIM
HERBERT R. KEITH
MICHAEL D. KELLEY
RICHARD A. KELLEY
ALPHONSO D. KEMP
STEVEN C. KEMP
RICHARD A. KERNES
LARRY W. KING
PATRICK D. KING
JERRY D. KIRTON
DANIEL I. KLEIN
THOMAS W. KLOIBER

JEFF J. KNAPP
PATRICK M. KNAPP
EDWARD L. KOCH, JR.
LEROY D. KOLAR
DARREN KONECHNEY
TERRY R. KONECHNEY
JERE D. KORTHANKE
KEVIN D. KRAUSE
JOHN G. KRIZER
JIMMY L. KRUTA
MICHAEL KRZYWDA
LEE A. KYLE
BETTY J. LAMB
BOBBY W. LAMBERT
JIMMY W. LAMBERT
RONALD D. LAMBERT
LESLIE LAMBETH
BRUCE W. LANDRY
DAVID J. LANDSBERGER
STEVEN E. LANE
KEVIN M. LANIER
JACE LARGENT
MICHAEL T. LATHAM
JAMES M. LAVASQUE
CHARLES S. LAW
TOMMY J. LAWRENCE
SANDRA LAWSON
ROBERT E. LAX, JR.
DAVID W. LAXTON
ROBERT L. LAYMON
ROGER N. LEAKE
LARRY M. LECK

MARK S. LEDLOW
ROBERT J. LEDLOW
KELLIE J. LEE
MICHELE LEE
NOBLE F. LEE
WILLIAM F. LEIBOLD
RAY K. LEMONS
TOMMY G. LEMONS
BOB LESTER, JR.
HAROLD D. LEVERETT
DAVID A. LEVESCY, JR.
BRANDON J. LEWIS
MARK A. LEWIS
TREVOR L. LEWIS
JOHN T. LIDDLE
STEVEN A. LINCOLN
GREGORY A. LINDSAY
LEONARD G. LINK
JERRY LITTERELL
JOANN LITTLE
JAMES M. LONG, II
JOHN H. LONG
TIMOTHY A. LONG
BRADLEY W. LOVE
KENNETH L. LOVELESS
RONALD L. LOVELESS
MELVIN L. LUMMUS
STEVEN B. LUMRY
LARRY W. LUNOW
RANDALL E. LUNOW
JAMES A. LUTZ
DAVID B. LYNCH

TIMOTHY C. LYTLE
TONY L. MACK
PEPPER L. MACKEY
JAY R. MAGERUS
MICHAEL S. MAHONEY
RANDALL L. MALONE
CURTIS R. MALOY
POWELL O. MANION
DOUGLAS L. MANNING
RICHARD W. MANUEL
JACK D. MAPLES
BOIS D. MARABLE
GARY R. MARLOW
GARY B. MARRS
LOUIS J. MARSCHIK
MICHAEL L. MARSHALL
ROBERT L. MARSHALL
ANTHONY MARTIN
PHILLIP S. MARTIN
RICHARD A. MARTIN
STEPHEN A. MARTINEZ
STEVEN P. MARTINEZ
CALVIN W. MASON
MARTIN T. MATTHEWS
WILLIAM C. MAUPIN
CURTIS W. MAYFIELD
DAVID J. MAYNARD
ROBERT D. MCAFEE
DANIEL L. MCALLISTER
DANIEL L. MCALLISTER, II
KEITH M. MCCABE
WILLIAM MCCAINE, III

DON W. MCCARTHEY
GARY L. MCCONNELL
LEWIS D. MCCONNELL
KURK R. MCCORNACK
DAVID N. MCCUDDY
LAJOHN MCDONALD
WILLIAM L. MCDONALD
LELAND C. MCELROY, JR.
DANNY MCEWIN
MICHAEL W. MCFARLAND
CHRISTOPHER MCKENZIE
TAMMY A. MCKINNEY
ROBERT H. MCMAHON
KEITH D. MCMURPHY
MICHAEL S. MCWHORTER
JAMEY MEADOWS
JAMES L. MEARS
MICHAEL MEDRANO
TERRY L. MEEKER
CECIL R. MEEKS
FARRELL H. MELTON
JIMMY D. MENEFEE
CHRISTY MEYER
DAVID R. MEYER
BRADLEY J. MICHAUD
ROBERT C. MIDDLETON
ANTHONY MILLER
BRIAN K. MILLER
MICHAEL A. MILLER
RICHARD C. MILLER
ROCKY D. MILLER
JERRY D. MILLS

JOEL R. MILNER
DONALD L. MING, JR.
DAVID G. MITCHELL
LEONARD G. MITCHELL
ROBERT W. MITCHELL
JOHN MOAD
MICHAEL L. MOAD
MARK R. MOLLMAN
MICHAEL P. MOONEY
OLIVER G. MOORE
FELTON MORGAN, III
TERRY G. MORTENSON
RONALD MOSS
BOBBY J. MOWLES, JR.
PAUL R. MUNGER
ANDRE E. MUNSEY
SAMUEL L. MUSICK
PAUL MUSKRAT
TERRY L. MYERS
LINDA A. NELLIS
MICHAEL P. NETTLETON
EARL DEAN NEWLUN
ROY NEWMAN
STEPHEN T. NEWMAN
WES A. NEWTON
DANA R. NICHOLS
NATHAN NICHOLS
GREGORY T. NICHOLSON
CHERRY A. NIPPERT
MICHAEL R. NITZEL
LOUIS A. NIX
ANTOINETTE M. NORMAN

LESLEY C. NORMAN
JAMES R. NORTHCUTT
REX L. O'BRIEN
DAVID G. O'KRESIK
EDDIE C. OAKS, JR.
ROBERT E. OLDHAM
KENNETH OLESON
DAVID W. OLIVER
WILLIAM O. ORR
SCOTT J. OSBAN
DAVID W. OWEN
JOHN D. PARASICH, JR.
STEVEN W. PARK
ANTHONY W. PARKER
LAVERNE M. PARKER
HARLEY G. PARKS
STEVEN PARKS
MATTHEW L. PASCHAL
MICHAEL S. PASCHAL
DONALD T. PAYNE
CARRIE L. PENNINGTON
MICHAEL R. PENNINGTON
MICHAEL T. PENNINGTON
STEPHEN L. PENNINGTON
EDWARD L. PERKINS
MARCUS L. PERNELL
BILLY M. PETERMAN
STEVEN B. PETERS
JEFFERY D. PHILLIPS
JOHN D. PHILLIPS
STEVE M. PHILLIPS
THOMAS A. PHILLIPS

MITCHELL T. PIERCE
MARY R. PIRRAGLIA
MICHAEL W. PITTS
BILLY D. PLUMLEE
JERAL A. PLUMLEE
ROCKY D. POLLOCK
RONALD PONDS
DOUGLAS G. POSTON
MATTHEW W. POWERS
COY M. PRATHER
DONALD G. PRICE
JERRY L. PRINCE
JONATHAN A. PROTZMAN
JONATHAN A. PRUITT
MARTY S. PRYOR
DUANE L. PUCKETT
KINLEY M. PURCELL
CARL A. PURSER
JERRY W. QUICK
FREDDIE W. RACHEL
MIKE D. RAGSDALE
RONALD W. RAINBOW
LINDA RAINS
CHARLES D. RAMIREZ
DAN M. RAMOS
DELBERT D. RAMSEY, II
TRACY D. RAPER
AHMED O. RASHIDI
TROY D. RAWLS, JR.
PHILLIP M. RAY
DAVID L. RECORD
ROBERT L. RECTOR

WILLIAM H. REDDING
KEVIN D. REECE
DUSTIN RENNER
JEFFREY D. RENNER
ROBERT W. RENNER
STEVEN T. RENSHAW
CLAUDE R. REX
JAMES A. REYNOLDS
RICHARD B. REYNOLDS
GARY D. RICHARDS
RAYMOND RICHARDS
HOBART RICHARDSON, JR.
MICHAEL R. RICHARDSON
MICHAEL W. RICHARDSON
TRACY L. RIDER
LARRY J. RIGSBY
KRISTI S. RILEY
KENNETH M. RINEHART
KENNETH RITCHIE
CARLA S. ROBERSON
CARROLL D. ROBERTS
GRANT W. ROBERTS
JOSEPH ROBERTS, JR.
LARRY J. ROBERTS
MICHAEL E. ROBERTS
QUINN L. ROBERTS
RONNIE D. ROBERTS
ANDREW K. ROBERTSON
BILL ROBINETT
ELLWOOD L. ROBINSON
KENNETH A. ROCKOW
CRAIG A. ROLKE

KENNETH P. ROLKE
RANDALL R. ROSE
ROY A. ROSS
JAMES RODNEY ROYS
LARRY D. RUSHER
BRYAN RUSSELL
RONALD A. RUYLE
MICHAEL L. RYCHLEC
RONNIE J. SALLEE
ROBERT L. SANDERS
AREY S. SAWYER
JAMES M. SCALF
HENRY F. SCHILLING
JIMMY D. SCHINER
DWIGHT A. SCHMIDT
RICHARD E. SCHMITT
JOHNNY R. SCHOFIELD
CRAIG L. SCHULTZ
GARY D. SCHWARTZ
JAY M. SCOTT
RICKIE L. SCOTT
RICHARD E. SCRIVNER
TERRY D. SCRIVNER
RICHARD W. SCROGGINS
MICHAEL W. SEATON
MICHAEL D. SEELEY
TERRELL D. SELBY
LARRY A. SELVEY
MICHAEL C. SEXTON
ROBERT M. SEYMOUR
BRITT L. SHANNON
MICHAEL L. SHANNON

CHRIS A. SHAW
PATRICK L. SHAW
NATHAN SHIPMAN
ANTHONY D. SHOCKLEY
RICHARD M. SHULTS
GLENDON N. SHUNKWILER
SHAWN P. SIMON
VERNON L. SIMPSON
GERALD P. SIPE, JR.
GARY D. SLATE
TOMMY D. SMART
ALPHONZO J. SMILEY
MICHAEL L. SMILEY
CORT K. SMITH
DWIGHT L. SMITH
ELZIE C. SMITH
JASON K. SMITH
JOE M. SMITH
KENNETH H. SMITH
MICHAEL L. SMITH
RICHARD A. SMITH
RONNIE D. SMITH
WHISPERN SMITH
MIKE O. SMOOT
GARY F. SNOW
JOHN A. SOOS
CURTIS R. SPEEGLE
SCOTTY D. SPENCE
DALE S. SPENCER
STEPHEN R. SPENCER
TODD S. SPENCER
JEFFREY S. SPIVA

GLASCO R. SPRIGGS
JOHN E. SPRINKLE, JR.
BRIAN STANALAND
JOE S. STANFORD, JR.
TROY W. STANFORD
DAVID B. STAPLES
BERT L. STARK
JOSHUA L. STARK
DETRICH L. STARR
DAVID STEELE
JEFFREY D. STEELE
BRYAN M. STEFFES
THOMAS M. STEGNER
H. DAVID STEVENS
LARRY K. STEVENSON
ARTIE P. STEWART
RICHARD L. STIGER
RICHARD D. STINER
CHARLES L. STONE
KEVIN W. STONEKING
BRYAN E. STORY
PAUL E. STRAUBE
SCOTT M. STROTHER
SHERRY D. STROTHER
STEVE T. STROTHER
RAYMOND J. STUART
DAVID H. SUBLETT
TRAVIS W. SULLIVAN
FARRIL A. SUMMERS
P. BRETT SUTTERFIELD
MARK A. SVETGOFF
THOMAS F. SWANSON

RICHARD D. SWINK
PAUL J. SWINNEY
JAN SYDNES
ANTHONY D. TABOR
JAMES W. TALKINGTON
HERBERT W. TANNER
JOHNNIE G. TATE
BRICE W. TAYLOR, JR.
JIMMY L. TAYLOR
NEIL A. TAYLOR
STEVE E. TAYLOR
STEVEN T. TAYLOR
TODD M. TAYLOR
JAMES K. TEAL
VERNON J. TENNILL
MICHAEL D. TENNYSON
DENNIE W. THOMAS
RANDEL K. THOMAS
DON W. THOMASON
CHRISTOPHER G. THOMPSON
DANIEL D. THOMPSON
HAROLD J. THOMPSON
HOMER J. THOMPSON
OLEN O. THOMPSON
TOMMY J. THOMPSON
ERIC R. THOMSEN
THOMAS A. THURM
GARY L. THURMAN
DANIEL E. TICE
MICHAEL W. TIDERMAN
SHAWN L. TIDWELL
WEBB A. TILTON

ROBERT TINDALL
WILLIAM TOBIN
RANDEL TOMPKINS
TONY TOMPKINS
J. DEWAYNE TORRES
TIMOTHY K. TOWNSEND
STEVEN A. TRIMBLE
ROY D. TRITTEN
DAVID J. TROWBRIDGE
MARIE TUBBS
DAVID R. TUCKER
RANDALL D. TUCKER
FRANK TURNER, JR.
ROBERT D. TURNER
ROOSEVELT TURNER, III
PAUL W. VAIL
STEPHEN A. VANDERBURG
RANDAL R. VANDIVER
SCOTT VANHORN
BERNARDO R. VASQUEZ
VICENTE VASQUEZ
RAY A. VELEZ
CALVIN L. VERNON
MICHAEL A. VERNON
RICHARD D. VERNON
RODNEY S. VERNON
MICHAEL S. VICSEK
MITCHEL J. VOLK
LARRY A. WADDLE
TERRY L. WADDLE
JAMES L. WAGGONER
LARRY WALKER

MICHAEL L. WALKER
TIMOTHY T. WALL
GERALD W. WALLACE
JIMMY L. WALLACE
TOBY L. WALSER
VICENTE L. WALTER
ROBERT M. WARCUP
ALLAN A. WARD
BARBARA WARD
JOSEPH D. WARD
TIMOTHY A. WARD
GREGORY S. WARLICK
LARRY WATSON
SAMUEL D. WATSON
JOHNNY R. WEATHERFORD
MICHAEL L. WEATHERLY
WALTER G. WEATHERLY
HARVEY L. WEATHERS, JR.
HUBERT WEAVER
TERRY G. WEAVER
TIMOTHY E. WEAVER
MICHAEL J. WEBB
ADAM M. WELLIVER
BRIAN C. WELLS
CHARLES J. WELLS
RICHARD S. WHEELER
STEVEN L. WHEELER
ROBERT L. WHEELUS
BRUCE W. WHITE
DARLENE R. WHITE
JEFFREY S. WHITE
SCOTT M. WHITE

BRAD WHITEHOUSE
TED WHITNAH
ERIC S. WHITT
DAVID R. WHOMBLE
ROBERT V. WILDER, JR.
ROBERT P. WILKERSON
DOUGLAS J. WILLIAMS
JAMES WILLIAMS
JAMES A. WILLIAMS
JOHN W. WILLIAMS
MARCUS P. WILLIAMS
MARCUS S. WILLIAMS
RICKY L. WILLIAMS
TROY L. WILLIAMS
WILLIAM M. WILLIAMS
ROBERT L. WILLIS
LUCKY D. WILSON
MANNING WILSON
NEVILLE R. WILSON
NORRIS A. WILSON
RICKY WILSON
STEVE M. WILSON
DON L. WINDLE
TERRY S. WINSTON
DARRELL D. WITT
RONALD E. WITT
GREG P. WOLF
ROY A. WOLF
DAVID R. WOMACK
CARL J. WOODARD
DON G. WOODARD
MARC L. WOODARD

OKLAHOMA RESCUE

WILLIAM L. WOODARD
KIMBERLYN K. WOODRING
RANDAL J. WOODS
SIDNEY N. WOODY
CHRIS M. WRIGHT
DOUGLAS E. WRIGHT
GERALD W. WRIGHT
KIRK D. WRIGHT
WILBUR D. WRIGHT
ERVIN E. WYATT
THOMAS D. YANCEY
JERRY L. YARBROUGH
RICK D. YARBROUGH
STEVE D. YORK
STEVEN R. YOSCAK
CORNELIUS L. YOUNG
GEORGE T. YOUNG
JAMES L. YOUNG
JOHN P. YOUNG
RONALD L. YOUNG
STEVEN R. YOUNG
TONY R. YOUNG

KILLED IN THE LINE OF DUTY MARCH 8, 1989

CAPTAIN JIMMY AYERS
CAPTAIN BENNY ZELLNER
FIREFIGHTER JEFF LINDSEY

The Federal Emergency Management Agency's Urban Search and Rescue teams involved in the Oklahoma City incident:

Fairfax County Fire and Rescue Department of Fairfax, Virginia

Los Angeles County Fire Department of Los Angeles, California

Menlo Park Fire Department of Menlo Park, California

Metro-Dade County Fire Department of Miami, Florida

Montgomery County Fire Department of Silver Spring, Maryland

New York Office of Emergency Management of New York

Orange County Fire Department of Orange County, California

Phoenix Fire Department of Phoenix, Arizona

Puget Sound Fire Department of Tacoma, Washington

Sacramento Fire Department of Sacramento, California

Virginia Beach Fire Department of Virginia Beach, Virginia

Readers who wish to learn more about the Oklahoma Firefighters Memorial Fund may write to:

2716 Northeast 50th Street
Oklahoma City, Oklahoma 73111

or phone: 1-405-424-1452